Percent of Accuracy Chart (20–190 Words)

To determine your percent of accuracy on a timed writing, locate the number of gross words you keyed in the first column.

Read across the top to locate the total number of errors you made. Then read down the column to find your percent of accuracy.

Example: If you keyed 103 words and made 4 errors, you would have keyed with 96.1 percent of accuracy.

AF691033

NO. OF GROSS WORDS	ERRORS (FROM 1 TO 15)														
	1	2	3	4	5	6	7	8	9	10	11	12	13	14	15
20–30	96.0	92.0	88.0	84.0	80.0	76.0	72.0	68.0	64.0	60.0					
31–35	97.0	93.9	90.9	87.9	84.8	81.8	78.8	75.8	72.7	69.7					
36–40	97.4	94.7	92.1	89.5	86.8	84.2	81.6	78.9	76.3	73.7					
41–45	97.7	95.3	93.0	90.7	88.4	86.0	83.7	81.4	79.1	76.7					
46–50	97.9	95.8	93.8	91.7	89.6	87.5	85.4	83.3	81.3	79.2					
51–55	98.1	96.2	94.3	92.5	90.6	88.7	86.8	84.9	83.0	81.1					
56–60	98.3	96.6	94.8	93.1	91.4	89.7	87.9	86.2	84.5	82.8					
61–65	98.4	96.8	95.2	93.7	92.1	90.5	88.9	87.3	85.7	84.1					
66–70	98.5	97.1	95.6	94.1	92.6	91.2	89.7	88.2	86.8	85.3					
71–75	98.6	97.3	95.9	94.5	93.2	91.8	90.4	89.0	87.7	86.3					
76–80	98.7	97.4	96.2	94.9	93.6	92.3	91.0	89.7	88.5	87.2					
81–85	98.8	97.6	96.4	95.2	94.0	92.8	91.6	90.4	89.2	88.0					
86–90	98.9	97.7	96.6	95.5	94.3	93.2	92.0	90.9	89.8	88.6					
91–95	98.9	97.8	96.8	95.7	94.6	93.5	92.5	91.4	90.3	89.2					
96–100	99.0	98.0	96.9	95.9	94.9	93.9	92.9	91.8	90.8	89.8					
101–105	99.0	98.1	97.1	96.1	95.1	94.2	93.2	92.2	91.3	90.3	89.3	88.3	87.3	86.4	85.4
106–110	99.1	98.1	97.2	96.3	95.4	94.4	93.5	92.6	91.7	90.7	89.8	88.8	88.0	87.0	86.1
111–115	99.1	98.2	97.3	96.5	95.6	94.7	93.8	92.9	92.0	91.2	90.3	89.4	88.5	87.6	86.7
116–120	99.2	98.3	97.5	96.6	95.8	94.9	94.1	93.2	92.4	91.5	90.7	89.8	89.0	88.1	87.3
121–125	99.2	98.4	97.6	96.7	95.9	95.1	94.3	93.5	92.7	91.9	91.0	90.2	89.4	88.6	87.8
126–130	99.2	98.4	97.7	96.9	96.1	95.3	94.5	93.8	93.0	92.2	91.4	90.6	89.8	89.1	88.3
131–135	99.2	98.5	97.7	97.0	96.2	95.5	94.7	94.0	93.2	92.5	91.7	91.0	90.2	89.5	88.7
136–140	99.3	98.6	97.8	97.1	96.4	95.7	94.9	94.2	93.5	92.8	92.0	91.3	90.6	89.9	89.1
141–145	99.3	98.6	97.9	97.2	96.5	95.8	95.1	94.4	93.7	93.0	92.3	91.6	90.9	90.2	89.5
146–150	99.3	98.6	98.0	97.3	96.6	95.9	95.3	94.6	93.9	93.2	92.6	91.9	91.2	90.5	89.9
151–155	99.3	98.7	98.0	97.4	96.7	96.1	95.4	94.8	94.1	93.5	92.8	92.2	91.5	90.8	90.2
156–160	99.4	98.7	98.1	97.5	96.8	96.2	95.6	94.9	94.3	93.7	93.0	92.4	91.8	91.1	90.5
161–165	99.4	98.8	98.2	97.5	96.9	96.3	95.7	95.1	94.5	93.9	93.3	92.6	92.0	91.4	90.8
166–170	99.4	98.8	98.2	97.6	97.0	96.4	95.8	95.2	94.6	94.0	93.5	92.9	92.3	91.7	91.0
171–175	99.4	98.8	98.3	97.7	97.1	96.5	96.0	95.4	94.8	94.2	93.6	93.1	92.5	91.9	91.3
176–180	99.4	98.9	98.3	97.8	97.2	96.6	96.1	95.5	94.9	94.4	93.8	93.3	92.7	92.1	91.6
181–185	99.5	98.9	98.4	97.8	97.3	96.7	96.2	95.6	95.1	94.5	94.0	93.4	93.0	92.3	91.8
186–190	99.5	98.9	98.4	97.9	97.3	96.8	96.3	95.7	95.2	94.7	94.1	93.6	93.1	92.6	92.0

Continued

© by the Glencoe Division of Macmillan/McGraw-Hill.

Percent of Accuracy Chart (191–400 Words)

NO. OF GROSS WORDS	ERRORS (FROM 1 TO 15)														
	1	2	3	4	5	6	7	8	9	10	11	12	13	14	15
191–195	99.5	99.0	98.4	97.9	97.4	96.9	96.4	95.9	95.3	94.8	94.3	93.8	93.3	92.7	92.2
196–200	99.5	99.0	98.5	98.0	97.5	97.0	96.5	96.0	95.5	94.9	94.4	93.9	93.4	92.9	92.4
201–205	99.5	99.0	98.5	98.0	97.5	97.0	96.6	96.1	95.6	95.1	94.6	94.0	93.6	93.1	92.6
206–210	99.5	99.0	98.6	98.1	97.6	97.1	96.6	96.2	95.7	95.2	94.7	94.2	93.8	93.3	92.8
211–215	99.5	99.1	98.6	98.1	97.7	97.2	96.7	96.2	95.8	95.3	94.8	94.4	93.9	93.4	93.0
216–220	99.5	99.1	98.6	98.2	97.7	97.2	96.8	96.3	95.9	95.4	95.0	94.5	94.0	93.6	93.1
221–225	99.6	99.1	98.7	98.2	97.8	97.3	96.9	96.4	96.0	95.5	95.1	94.6	94.2	93.7	93.2
226–230	99.6	99.1	98.7	98.2	97.8	97.4	96.9	96.5	96.1	95.6	95.2	94.7	94.3	93.9	93.4
231–235	99.6	99.1	98.7	98.3	97.9	97.4	97.0	96.6	96.1	95.7	95.3	94.8	94.4	94.0	93.6
236–240	99.6	99.2	98.7	98.3	97.9	97.5	97.1	96.6	96.2	95.8	95.4	95.0	94.5	94.1	93.7
241–245	99.6	99.2	98.8	98.4	97.9	97.5	97.1	96.7	96.3	95.9	95.5	95.1	94.7	94.2	93.8
246–250	99.6	99.2	98.8	98.4	98.0	97.6	97.2	96.8	96.4	96.0	95.6	95.2	94.8	94.4	94.0
251–255	99.6	99.2	98.8	98.4	98.0	97.6	97.2	96.8	96.4	96.0	95.7	95.3	94.9	94.5	94.1
256–260	99.6	99.2	98.8	98.4	98.1	97.7	97.3	96.9	96.5	96.1	95.7	95.3	95.0	94.6	94.2
261–265	99.6	99.2	98.9	98.5	98.1	97.7	97.3	97.0	96.6	96.2	95.8	95.4	95.1	94.7	94.3
266–270	99.6	99.3	98.9	98.5	98.1	97.8	97.4	97.0	96.6	96.3	95.9	95.5	95.1	94.8	94.4
271–275	99.6	99.3	98.9	98.5	98.2	97.8	97.4	97.1	96.7	96.3	96.0	95.6	95.2	94.9	94.5
276–280	99.6	99.3	98.9	98.6	98.2	97.8	97.5	97.1	96.8	96.4	96.0	95.7	95.3	95.0	94.6
281–285	99.6	99.3	98.9	98.6	98.2	97.9	97.5	97.2	96.8	96.5	96.1	95.8	95.4	95.1	94.7
286–290	99.7	99.3	99.0	98.6	98.3	97.9	97.6	97.2	96.9	96.5	96.2	95.8	95.5	95.1	94.8
291–295	99.7	99.3	99.0	98.6	98.3	98.0	97.6	97.3	96.9	96.6	96.2	95.9	95.6	95.2	94.9
296–300	99.7	99.3	99.0	98.7	98.3	98.0	97.7	97.3	97.0	96.6	96.3	96.0	95.6	95.3	95.0
301–305	99.7	99.3	99.0	98.7	98.3	98.0	97.7	97.4	97.0	96.7	96.4	96.0	95.7	95.4	95.0
306–310	99.7	99.4	99.0	98.7	98.4	98.1	97.7	97.4	97.1	96.8	96.4	96.1	95.8	95.5	95.1
311–315	99.7	99.4	99.0	98.7	98.4	98.1	97.8	97.4	97.1	96.8	96.5	96.2	95.8	95.5	95.2
316–320	99.7	99.4	99.1	98.7	98.4	98.1	97.8	97.5	97.2	96.9	96.5	96.2	95.9	95.6	95.3
321–325	99.7	99.4	99.1	98.8	98.5	98.1	97.8	97.5	97.2	96.9	96.6	96.3	96.0	95.7	95.4
326–330	99.7	99.4	99.1	98.8	98.5	98.2	97.9	97.6	97.3	97.0	96.6	96.3	96.0	95.7	95.4
331–335	99.7	99.4	99.1	98.8	98.5	98.2	97.9	97.6	97.3	97.0	96.7	96.4	96.1	95.8	95.5
336–340	99.7	99.4	99.1	98.8	98.5	98.2	97.9	97.6	97.3	97.0	96.7	96.4	96.2	95.9	95.6
341–345	99.7	99.4	99.1	98.8	98.5	98.3	98.0	97.7	97.4	97.1	96.8	96.5	96.2	95.9	95.6
346–350	99.7	99.4	99.1	98.9	98.6	98.3	98.0	97.7	97.4	97.1	96.8	96.6	96.3	96.0	95.7
351–355	99.7	99.4	99.2	98.9	98.6	98.3	98.0	97.7	97.5	97.2	96.9	96.6	96.3	96.0	95.8
356–360	99.7	99.4	99.2	98.9	98.6	98.3	98.0	97.8	97.5	97.2	96.9	96.6	96.4	96.1	95.8
361–365	99.7	99.4	99.2	98.9	98.6	98.3	98.1	97.8	97.5	97.2	97.0	96.7	96.4	96.1	95.9
366–370	99.7	99.5	99.2	98.9	98.6	98.4	98.1	97.8	97.6	97.3	97.0	96.7	96.5	96.2	95.9
371–375	99.7	99.5	99.2	98.9	98.7	98.4	98.1	97.9	97.6	97.3	97.1	96.8	96.5	96.2	96.0
376–380	99.7	99.5	99.2	98.9	98.7	98.4	98.1	97.9	97.6	97.4	97.1	96.8	96.6	96.3	96.0
381–385	99.7	99.5	99.2	99.0	98.7	98.4	98.2	97.9	97.7	97.4	97.1	96.9	96.6	96.3	96.1
386–390	99.7	99.5	99.2	99.0	98.7	98.5	98.2	97.9	97.7	97.4	97.2	96.9	96.6	96.4	96.1
391–395	99.7	99.5	99.2	99.0	98.7	98.5	98.2	98.0	97.7	97.5	97.2	96.9	96.7	96.4	96.2
396–400	99.7	99.5	99.2	99.0	98.7	98.5	98.2	98.0	97.7	97.5	97.2	97.0	96.7	96.5	96.2

© by the Glencoe Division of Macmillan/McGraw-Hill.

Technique Rating Sheet

At various times, rate yourself on each of these techniques.

SCORING:

Excellent = 4 points
Good = 3 points
Average = 2 points
Poor = 1 point

TECHNIQUE GOAL Technique Cue	RATING PERIOD 1	2	3	4	5	6	7	8
Position the body properly With the elbows in a natural position, sit so the fingers are curved properly over home-key position; keep elbows by your sides, but not touching your body; rest your back against the back of the chair								
Position feet properly Place feet flat on the floor and slightly apart; one foot slightly in front of the other								
E T Insert paper efficiently Pull paper bail/insertion lever forward; rest paper evenly behind the platen; feed the paper into the machine using the automatic paper insert or by turning the platen knob until paper is in position; check alignment of paper; push paper bail/insertion lever back; begin keying immediately................								
M Insert disk efficiently Open the door to the disk drive; hold program disk with the label facing up; insert program disk into Drive 1 and close the door; insert student disk into Drive 2 and close the door; turn on the monitor; turn on the microcomputer; follow screen prompts...............................								
Use proper wrist and finger position Keep the wrists low but not touching the equipment; rotate wrists inward so that fingers are in a direct, vertical line with the keys; curve the fingers; do not bounce the wrists.................................								
Keep stroking action in the fingers Hold the wrists and arms almost motionless; make reaches with the fingers—not with the hands and arms; strike each key with a quick, sharp stroke; snap the finger toward the palm after each stroke								
Key by touch Do not look at your fingers as you key; keep your eyes on the copy...................								

Continued

© by the Glencoe Division of Macmillan/McGraw-Hill.

Technique Rating Sheet

SCORING:

Excellent = 4 points
Good = 3 points
Average = 2 points
Poor = 1 point

TECHNIQUE GOAL Technique Cue	RATING PERIOD 1	2	3	4	5	6	7	8
Key without pauses Do not pause between letters or words; try to keep the carrier/cursor moving; key easy-to-stroke two- and three-letter combinations rapidly; slow down for difficult reaches; key some words as words rather than as separate letters.								
Space properly Use a quick down-and-in tapping motion of the right thumb; space between words without pausing; let the side of the thumb lightly touch the space bar; do not space at the end of a line.								
Return the carrier/cursor properly Press the return/enter key lightly with the **sem** finger and release quickly; return to home-key position immediately; keep other fingers in home-key position; keep eyes on the copy throughout the return/enter operation; do not space before returning; begin keying the next line without a pause								
Use shift keys properly Use a one-two count as (1) the **a** or **sem** finger presses the shift and (2) the key is struck with the opposite hand; keep other fingers over home-key position; quickly release the shift key and return finger to home-key position; keep eyes on copy								
Tabulate properly Make a finger reach to the tab key; keep the wrist low; avoid up-and-down hand movement; keep eyes on copy; key as soon as the carrier/cursor reaches the tab setting								
E T Remove paper efficiently Pull paper bail/insertion lever toward you; operate the paper-release lever; pull paper out of machine; turn off the typewriter . . .								
M Remove disk efficiently Follow screen prompts; store document; wait for red light on disk drive to go off; open door to disk drive; remove the disk, and place it in the protective envelope; turn off the power to the monitor and the microcomputer.								
TOTAL POINTS								

© by the Glencoe Division of Macmillan/McGraw-Hill.

NAME DATE CLASS

Keyboard Practice

SS or default

SM: Default or 1″

Key each group of drill lines. Return/enter and key the lines again.

DS Continue with the remaining groups of drill lines.

LESSON 2

asdf jkl; a; sl dk fj ;a ls kd jf a;a sls dkd fjfj
aa ;; ss ll dd kk ff jj fj dk sl a; ;lkj jf; fdsa;
aj ak al fj fk fl la ls ld kd dl ka ks ;f s; as df

sad; fad; ask; all; lad; lass; dad; fall fad; lad;
lad fall sad ;lass ask; dad; lads; all dads a fall
;ask; a dad; fall; sad lass all lads; sad dad lass

a lad; as sad as; lad a; lass asks; all fall; dads
dads all fall; ask all lads; as sad as a lad; lass
sad lass; ask dad; all sad lads; falls; ask a lass

LESSON 3

E ded deed deaf deal seed led ade dale dell lead eel
ded seed feed ease seas fad feel keel jell fee elf
ded sea; sell; desk; jell; keel; deaf; fees; fade;

H jhj hadj sash has aha half had hall dash shall ash
jhj sash haj lash halls shall hah hajj hallah shah
jhj shad; dah; kaka; ha ha; has; had; hall; shall;

T ftf fat fast daft fatal staff last flat talk salts
ftf salt tall staffs fasts flats lasts talks stalk
ftf stall; tad; taj; fate; task; sat; staff; fast;

LESSON 4

I kik like kid dike silk kites hike sheik khaki kiss
kik hit did hid fit lilt tilt this sift list jilts
kik said; fists; hiss; dishes; fish; hiked; liked;

G fgf gaffe flag gag gale get glass egg hag gas gate
fgf tagged sag sage leg gassed keg jagged gad gaff
fgf; gadget; gage; gala; gall; gel; age; lag; tag;

N jnj jeans handle stand end lank and tent lend sent
jnj neat nest ten tan need kneel needle knees teen
jnj fasten; fan; sand; hand; send; den; fend; hens

© by the Glencoe Division of Macmillan/McGraw-Hill.

Keyboard Practice Continued

SS or default

SM: Default or 1″

Key each group of drill lines. Return/enter and key the lines again.

DS Continue with the remaining groups of drill lines.

LESSON 6

O
lol long load look hole told soil loaf solo loosen
lol loin gone foil done soon hotel toast join oils
lol old off oaf odd oak ode of offense offset joke

R
frf fir far fear fire frets fair friend raft rifle
frf fright right resist reign rise rest rile rides
frf free grid lark kraft edger ridge rig jerk grad

SHIFT
Nan Helen Jane Kate India King Latin Jake Len Hank
Janet Jensen; Lana Jenkins; Hal Henning; Nan Neish
Late Night Last Lake Light Jest Isle High Its Idle

LESSON 7

U
juj jug jute jungle junk juggle jaguar just junket
juj judge us use hurts nut lug runs hunt dust hung
juj sung Lunt dour Kuhn gunner Judd hunter Lurner;

W
sws sweets waist news swing tows sewn straw swords
sws swear swish swag swoon swell swine swirl swore
sws twist twin twain twill two twine twig twilight

.
l.l Ltd. kg. Ill. Jr. Okla. ital. Ore. in. La. lg.
Look at orig. and ordn. Hire her. Let her learn.
It is Id.; it is not Ida. It is either in. or ft.

LESSON 9

P
;p; pep; people; whip; pear; pepper; pipe; sipped;
;p; pen; pet; pest; pig; poor; pure; pat; pad; pun
;p; whip wipe trip gulp loop swipe grip top ripple

,
k,k king, link, walk, tank, thanks, take, talking,
k,k kid, kill, kiln, kilt, kin, kind, king, kiosk,
k,k like, hike, rook, sake, fork, lake, joke, link

SHIFT
Rita Andrew Susan Delta Frank Ed Tulane Wales Greg
Tues. Wed. Thurs. Fri. Sat. Sun. August Washington
Tell Ed to go to Delhi. Wes and Don want Western.

© by the Glencoe Division of Macmillan/McGraw-Hill.

Keyboard Practice Continued

SS or default

SM: Default or 1″

Key each group of drill lines. Return/enter and key the lines again.

DS Continue with the remaining groups of drill lines.

LESSON 10

```
(M) jmj jam major jump jasmine jetsam summer main time
    jmj mere mist made mom must merit mama memo moment
    jmj home, him, swim, roam, omen, imminent, immense

(C) dcd deck cad scored dice credit duct dunce succeed
    dcd care clean circus cost cure caucus cricket cut
    dcd rich; church; French; Uncle; Dick; Nick; Chris

(Q) aqa aqua quart quota equal quaff quake squad qualm
    aqa quite quarter quell quip quirt quote quotation
    aqa He questioned the quotes.  I quoted the queen.
```

LESSON 12

```
(B) fbf fib fable fiber buff baffle forbid flab fabric
    fbf bad bed bid barque bud bake been bird bog burn
    fbf Brad brought Bob both big bottles before noon.

(Y) jyj joy Joey jelly jay July jetty juicy jury jolly
    jyj yes yeah yard yield Yule yucca Yukon yoke yelp
    jyj Gray, Yiddish, Terry, Tyler, quickly, quietly,

(X) sxs six taxes exist expense sax sexton waxes mixes
    sxs exhort expire exempt excuse expel extent extol
    sxs Tex expected six extras.  Rex explored Mexico.
```

LESSON 13

```
(V) fvf five favor fever verify fervor festive forever
    fvf veto Victor victim Virginia visa vivid Vietnam
    fvf have Vivian brave vex savor vixen vivify Virgo

(Z) aza glaze amaze adze haze lazy zeta Brazil Arizona
    aza Zion zest Zeus zero zoom Zuni zany Zulu zombie
    aza Zane spoke Zapotec.  Firenze dozed at the zoo.
```

© by the Glencoe Division of Macmillan/McGraw-Hill.

Keyboard Practice Continued

SS or default

SM: Default or 1″

Key each group of drill lines. Return/enter and key the lines again.

DS Continue with the remaining groups of drill lines.

LESSON 17

[:]

;:; Dear Kathy: Gentlemen: Add these: This way:
;:; Dear Zenos: Dear Verl: Dear Rex: Dear Brad:
;:; Send these three: File these: Ladies: Jack:

[?]

;?; What? When? How? Where? Is he? Will they?
;?; How many? What kinds? Whose is it? Why not?
;?; Write them? Why? Why not? Yes? No? Maybe?

LESSON 18

Keyboard 1 [']

;'; let's; wasn't; Jan's; you'll; can't; couldn't;
;'; it's, who's, shouldn't, she's, what's, that's,
;'; Rexroth's Levine's L'Enfant's Quezon's Ohlin's

Keyboard 2

j'j Jan's Kathy's Mike's Jenny's Lisa's I'm aren't
j'j Julie's you'll we'll John's Laura's isn't I'll
j'j Jethro's can't won't wouldn't Jane's Suzanne's

[-]

;-; first-class; self-made; thirty-four; all-star;
;-; vi-o-let, Yan-kee, Zech-a-ri-ah, xe-rog-ra-phy
;-; up-to-the-minute report; one-in-a-million lady

[LOCK] or All caps command

The ZIP Code abbreviations are OK, AZ, TX, and FL.
Two groups, UNRRA and UNRWA, were not represented.
N.A.A.; the TESOL group; the ILGWU; the I.L.G.W.U.

LESSON 19

Keyboard 1 ["]

;"; "loser" "always" "some" "perhaps" "only" "but"
;"; "Mdm." "FNMA" "Mex." "FYI" "d.b.a." "Nazareth"
;"; "Freddie" "Bob" "Marylu" "Johnny" "Ike" "Zeke"

Keyboard 2

s"s "she" "sure" "best" "thanks" "star" "sensible"
s"s "saw" "sing" "friend" "way" "ask" "goal" "are"
s"s "style" "Sarah" "computer" "run" "away" "twin"

Keyboard 1 [-] or Automatic underscore

;_; I am; the word like; Time; your book; one year
;_; I like Out of the Best Books and The Prophets.
;_; The LSAT? The GMAT? The SAT? USDA and USSR?

© by the Glencoe Division of Macmillan/McGraw-Hill.

NAME DATE CLASS

Keyboard Practice Continued

SS or default

SM: Default or 1″

Key each group of drill lines. Return/enter and key the lines again.

DS Continue with the remaining groups of drill lines.

LESSON 23

2 s2s 2 sides; 22 sons; 222 signs; 2,222 sets; 22.22
s2s 22 answers; 22 verses; 22 reports; 22 articles
s2s 22 foxes, 22.2 inches, 2,222 times, 22 sermons

3 d3d 3 dogs; 33 dimes; 333 dials; 3,333 deeds; 3.33
d3d 33 zeros, Quiz 33, 333 toys, 33 sixes, 33 yips
d3d 33.3 in.; 3.33 cm; 3.3 feet; 33.3 ft.; 3.33 gm

4 f4f 4 fires; 4.4 feet; 4,444 forts; 444 faces; 4.4
f4f File 44, No. 444, Exam 4, Try 44.4, Part 4,444
f4f 44 rooms; 44 doors; 4 fans; 44 steps; 44 knobs

LESSON 24

7 j7j 7 jugs; 77 jokes; 7,777 jewels; 777 jumps; 7.7
j7j July 7, Jogger 77, Jet 777, 7.77 mm, 77.77 in.
j7j 77 days; 77 months; 7 minutes; 77.7 hours; 7.7

8 k8k 8 kegs; 888 kilts; 8,888 keys; 88 kites; 88.88
k8k 8,888 miles, 888 km, 8.8 lbs., 8 in., 888 yds.
k8k Job 88; 888 kinds; 88.8 rods; 8 knots; 888 ft.

9 l9l 9 lots; 99 loans; 9,999 logs; 999 lists; 99.99
l9l 9 laps, Lot 99, Line 99.9, Lesson 99, 99 miles
l9l 9,999 times; 99 events; 99.9 percent; 9 inches

LESSON 26

1 a1a 1 act; 11 ads; 1,111 acres; 111 acids; 1.1 a1p
a1a Act 1, 11 answers, 1,111 miles, No. 111, 11 cm
a1a 1.11 mm; 111 reasons; 11.1 in.; 1 percent; 111

0 ;0; 30 days; 400 films; 7,000 bats; 20,000 leagues
;0; 10, 20, 30, 40, 70, 80, 90, 100, 200, 300, 400
;0; No. 10; 300 times; 0.03 in.; Line 20; 80 miles

$ f$f $9.99; $33.44; $223.99; $89.98; $72.49; $77.79
f$f $1.23, $2.34, $3.47, $4.89, $1.78, $9.89, $234
f$f $1; $2; $3; $4; $7; $8; $9; $11; $11 $11; $999

© by the Glencoe Division of Macmillan/McGraw-Hill.

Keyboard Practice Continued

SS or default

SM: Default or 1″

Key each group of drill lines. Return/enter and key the lines again.

DS Continue with the remaining groups of drill lines.

LESSON 27

5
f5f 5 figs; 55 flares; 5,555 fleas; 555 fads; 5.55
f5f 55 fives, 555 fires, No. 5, 5,555 mi., 55 boys
f5f 55.55 m; 5.5 in.; Line 55; 555 times; 555 lbs.

6
j6j 6 jars; 66 jays; 666 juries; 6,666 jumps; 6.66
j6j Job 66, No. 666, 6,666 miles; 66.6 in., 6 lbs.
j6j Jet 666; just 66.6; 6 times; No. 6,666; 666 cm

%
f%f 44%; 99.9%; 24%; 100%; 33%; 80%; 10%; 43%; 88%
f%f 1%, 2%, 3%, 4%, 5%, 6%, 7%, 8%, 9%, 100%, 200%
f%f 19%; 28%; 37%; 46%; 55%; 65%; 74%; 83%; 92% 1%

LESSON 29

Keyboard 1)
;); 1) I chose; 2) you chose; 3) he, she, it chose
;); 22) yes; ;); 33) no; ;); 44) maybe; 4) always;
;); 9) once; 10) twice; 28) true; 30) false; 7) no

Keyboard 2
l)l local) label) full) vertical) mall) all) goal)
l)l level) final) helpful) tall) trail) sail) ill)
l)l literal) little) moral) older) local) overall)

Keyboard 1 (
l(l (local) (lucky) (lulu) (little) (lately) (lot)
l(l (lines) (land) (lists) (laps) (loans) (little)
l(l (22); (23); (24); (25); (26); (27); (28); (29)

Keyboard 2
k(k (knock) (koala) (knight) (knots) (know) (knit)
k(k (knee) (knob) (knuckle) (kyack) (kudos) (kite)
k(k (44); (89); (54); (345); (21); (307); (5,722);

/
;/; either/or yes/no on/off left/right July/August
;/; one/two, 2/3, single/double, 3/4, up/down, 7/8
;/; 1/2; 5/6; 8/9; 1/10; 3/10; 7/10; 4/5; 4/7; 5/8

© by the Glencoe Division of Macmillan/McGraw-Hill.

NAME DATE CLASS

Word Scale Practice ACTIVITY 3 (Use after Lesson 11)

Use the text at the right to answer the questions that follow.

Check your answers on p. 89.

	1′	3′
In recent years, the computer revolution has been	10	3
taking place all around us. Like other revolutions before	22	7
it, this one affects us all, whether we know it or not and	34	11
whether we like it or not. We cannot escape the computer.	46	15
It is everywhere. It is found in the business world, in	57	19
education, in science, in law enforcement, in agriculture,	69	23
and in the home. After you become skillful using the	80	27
computer, you will understand how much it can do.	89	30

1′ | 1 | 2 | 3 | 4 | 5 | 6 | 7 | 8 | 9 | 10 | 11 | 12 | AWL
3′ | 1 | 2 | 3 | 4 | 5.7

What is your GWAM in each of the following situations?

1. In a 1-minute timing, you keyed through the word *business* in line 5? ______
2. In a 1-minute timing, you keyed the entire paragraph? ______
3. In a 3-minute timing, you keyed the entire paragraph once and through the word whether in line 3? ______
4. In a 3-minute timing, you keyed the paragraph once and reached the word *understand* in line 8? ______

© by the Glencoe Division of Macmillan/McGraw-Hill.

NAME DATE CLASS

Word Scale Practice ACTIVITY 1 (Use after Lesson 11)

Use the text at the right to answer the questions that follow.

Check your answers on p. 89.

	1′
He was told to check my test thoroughly.	8
Please do the important jobs accurately.	16
After the first day, he liked this work.	24
Before leaving tonight, please call her.	32
Jane took a keyboarding class this year.	40
Lonny finished each job before stopping.	48

| 1 | 2 | 3 | 4 | 5 | 6 | 7 | 8 |

1. If you key all of line 1, what is your GWAM? ______
2. If you key all six lines, what is your GWAM? ______
3. If you key all of line 1 and through the word *jobs* in line 2, what is your GWAM? ______
4. If you key all of lines 1, 2, and 3 and through the word *leaving* in line 4, what is your GWAM? ______
5. If you key all of the first five lines and through the word *before* in line 6, what is your GWAM? ______

© by the Glencoe Division of Macmillan/McGraw-Hill.

NAME DATE CLASS

Word Scale Practice ACTIVITY 4 (Use after Lesson 11)

Use the text at the right to answer the questions that follow.

Check your answers on p. 89.

	1′	3′
Computers can, through the highly advanced use of some	11	4
very small circuitry, use a set of orders to accept data in	23	8
the form of letters, figures, and symbols. Then, almost	35	12
all at once, they can process all the data into a useful	46	15
form. Computers come in lots of sizes. The large ones,	57	19
that have a great deal of storage and processing capacity,	69	23
are usually known as mainframes. The small ones are	80	27
called micros.	83	28

1′ | 1 | 2 | 3 | 4 | 5 | 6 | 7 | 8 | 9 | 10 | 11 | 12 | AWL

3′ | 1 | 2 | 3 | 4 | 5.7

What is your GWAM in each of the following situations?

1. In a 1-minute timing, you keyed through the end of line 5? ______
2. In a 3-minute timing, you keyed the paragraph once and reached the word *computers* in line 5? ______
3. In a 3-minute timing, you keyed the paragraph twice? ______
4. In a 3-minute timing, you keyed the paragraph twice and keyed through the word *circuitry* in line 2? ______

© by the Glencoe Division of Macmillan/McGraw-Hill.

NAME DATE CLASS

Word Scale Practice ACTIVITY 2 (Use after Lesson 11)

Use the text at the right to answer the questions that follow.

Check your answers on p. 89.

	1′
Use those good keying techniques you have learned.	10
You will find good keyboarding skills get results.	20
Keeping good posture will help you reduce fatigue.	30
The habit of eyes on the copy will increase speed.	40
Good techniques develop keying speed and accuracy.	50
Practice keyboarding whenever you have the chance.	60

| 1 | 2 | 3 | 4 | 5 | 6 | 7 | 8 | 9 | 10 |

1. If you keyed all six lines and through the word *keying* in line 1, what is your GWAM? ______
2. If you keyed all six lines twice and through the word *keying* in line 1, what is your GWAM? ______
3. If you keyed through the word *will* in line 4, what is your GWAM? ______
4. If you keyed all six lines and through the word *posture* in line 3, what is your GWAM? ______
5. If you keyed through the word *whenever* in line 6, what is your GWAM? ______

© by the Glencoe Division of Macmillan/McGraw-Hill.

NAME DATE CLASS

Misstroke Location Practice (Use after Lesson 15)

SS or default

SM: Default or 1″

If necessary, refer to Need to Know, 14E, in the textbook.

For each group of sentences at the right, the kind of misstroke is indicated. Circle the misstrokes in the sentences. Then, key each sentence correctly.

Check your answers on p. 89.

ACTIVITY 1 Omitted Letter(s)

Joe quicly proofread three term paers.

Reaching agreemen was a real necesity.

Janice needed mor time or keyboarding.

ACTIVITY 2 Omitted Word(s)

Ms. Brandt will another test today.

Yes, she finished assignments early.

Paul gave her one apple two peaches.

ACTIVITY 3 Added Letter(s)

The computer printout willl ben due today.

Too gain skill, your must always practice.

Do not forget too let Barb know thee rule.

ACTIVITY 4 Added Word(s)

The disk is not not currently in in this drive.

Andy knew his his answers were were all accurate.

Tanya left as as soon as she she finished work.

ACTIVITY 5 Review of Activities 1–4

As you input information, try concenrate on your workk. When your wanders, you tend to to make errrors. Emploers usuallly expect a employee too produce doccuments that are error freee. Correctting errors time cconsuming. Having spent timen makin correctionss can result lower productivity. Lower producttivity often resullts in lower profit for for the employe. Profit is important too any employer. No employer wil permit an employyee to contrbute to lowerin profits indefiniteely.

ACTIVITY 6 Extra Space

To re duce mis strokes, use concentra tion.

Per fect practice of fers perfect result s.

Concen tration is neces sary for accuracy.

Continued

© by the Glencoe Division of Macmillan/McGraw-Hill.

NAME DATE CLASS

Misstroke Location Practice Continued

SS or default

SM: Default or 1″

If necessary, refer to Need to Know, 14E, in the textbook.

For each group of sentences at the right, the kind of misstroke is indicated. Circle the misstrokes in the sentences. Then, key each sentence correctly.

Check your answers on p. 89.

ACTIVITY 7 No Space

Karl always usedgood keying techniques.

Eliminatefatigue by usinggood posture.

Always letyour eyes remain onthebook.

ACTIVITY 8 Misstroke

John proofreed carifully to find errers.

Make neet corrections on als misstroles.

Find and corrict tee 10 mistrokes here.

ACTIVITY 9 Transposition

Accurate keying si required for hte job.

Your wokr is always naet and error fere.

Taek pride daily ni het work yuo produce.

ACTIVITY 10 Strikeover

Set high standards and work toward them.

You'll feel proud when you reach a goal.

Set goals which reflect these standards.

ACTIVITY 11 Review Activities 6–9

You should always planyour assignment befere you begin. This mens taking tim to reed your instfuctions ande gather material and supplies you'l nead. Make cetrain yuo under stand all aspects fo the jbo beforebeginning work. You can waset valuabel tine and effort fi you haev to redo a job because youdid not underatand wha t het task involvde. Effective emploeyes adk questions to claer up nay prob lems beforethey begin to werk no a taks.Understanding what needs to bedone before startnig is veyr important. Youmight be very embarrassde and furstrated wneh you have todo a jbo again simply be cause you failedto under stand all the instrcutions.

© by the Glencoe Division of Macmillan/McGraw-Hill.

NAME DATE CLASS

Goal Writing Practice ACTIVITY 3

Compare the text at the right with the goal writing in 28C in the text.

Assume that you have keyed this text and made the errors shown. Circle all the errors that you find. Then, determine your GWAM, and record your accuracy.

Check your answers on p. 90.

	1′	3′
Computer systems are made up of sevreal	8	3
components; computer, keyboard, screen, printer,	18	6
and disk drive. The key-board is used to enter	28	9
data in to the computer. Data may be viewed on	37	12
the screen or sent to to the printer. Data is	46	15
store on floppy disks using the Disk drive. A	55	18
computer system is useful only when you have	64	21
Software that tells the computer what to do.	73	24

1′ | 1 | 2 | 3 | 4 | 5 | 6 | 7 | 8 | 9 | 10 |
3′ | 1 | 2 | 3 |

AWL 5.7

GWAM 1′ ______ Accuracy 1′ ______

3′ ______ 3′ ______

© by the Glencoe Division of Macmillan/McGraw-Hill.

NAME DATE CLASS

Goal Writing Practice ACTIVITY 1

Compare the text at the right with the goal writing in 19H in the text.

Assume that you have keyed this text and made the errors shown. Circle all the errors that you find. Then, determine your GWAM, and record your accuracy.

Check your answers on p. 89.

	1′	3′
Keting by touch means that you arecapable of	9	3
striking the keys with out looking at your fingers.	20	7
A distinctive Trait of outstanding keyboarders si	30	10
their ability to by key touch.	36	12
You should presently be keying nearly al of	45	15
your work by touch. Seldom should you have to to	54	18
glance at your fingers Instances when you have	64	21
to look down should be few and far between.	73	24

1′ | 1 | 2 | 3 | 4 | 5 | 6 | 7 | 8 | 9 | 10 |
3′ | 1 | 2 | 3 |

AWL 5.7

GWAM 1′ ______ Accuracy 1′ ______

3′ ______ 3′ ______

© by the Glencoe Division of Macmillan/McGraw-Hill.

NAME DATE CLASS

Goal Writing Practice ACTIVITY 4

Compare the text at the right with the goal writing in 31D in the textbook.

Assume that you have keyed this text and made the errors shown. Circle all the errors that you find. Then, determine your GWAM, and record your accuracy.

Check your answers on p. 90.

	1′	3′
A Typical day for a social worker involves	9	3
helping people identify and to solve their	18	6
problems. To be effective, a social worker must	28	9
be sensitive, yet objective at the same time.	37	12
A bachelor's degree is often needed for	45	15
entry level jobs. Many states give School grants to	55	18
to thoose workers who want to earn masters'	64	21
degree and to advance in their careers.	72	24

1′ | 1 | 2 | 3 | 4 | 5 | 6 | 7 | 8 | 9 | 10 | 11 | AWL 5.7
3′ | 1 | 2 | 3 | 4

GWAM 1′ ______ Accuracy 1′ ______

3′ ______ 3′ ______

© by the Glencoe Division of Macmillan/McGraw-Hill.

NAME DATE CLASS

Goal Writing Practice ACTIVITY 2

Compare the text at the right with the goal writing in 25C in the textbook.

Assume that you have keyed this text and made the errors shown. Circle all the errors that you find. Then, determine your GWAM, and record your accuracy.

Check your answers on p. 90.

	1′	3′
advances in technology have changed teh job	9	3
market. Some fields foemployment have been	18	6
eliminated while others have ben created.	27	9
What the world of work will be like in the	35	12
year to come will depend on the changes in	44	15
Technology. When you select a career try to	53	18
chose one that will allow some flexibility	63	21
to meet the changes in technology.	70	23

1′ | 1 | 2 | 3 | 4 | 5 | 6 | 7 | 8 | 9 | 10 | AWL 5.7
3′ | 1 | 2 | 3

GWAM 1′ ______ Accuracy 1′ ______

3′ ______ 3′ ______

© by the Glencoe Division of Macmillan/McGraw-Hill.

NAME DATE CLASS

Accuracy Practice (Use after Lesson 13)

SS or default

SM: Default or 1″

These sentences contain letter combinations that are either common in keyboarding or are difficult to key.

Practice those sentences containing letter combinations that you find troublesome.

Key each line at a comfortable pace. If you make an error, start again, keying more slowly. Stay on a line until you have keyed it without error.

a/e 1 Dean dealt with Beatrice when she ate the peaches and pears.

a/s 2 Sean plans to ask several salesmen to speak at his art show.

b/e 3 The ebony table and benches belong to Bevan and Betty Beebe.

b/n 4 The Nibley Benefit Banquet has been beneficial for Benjamin.

c/d 5 Dick condemned every codicil that Darcy dictated to Candice.

c/h 6 Teach each child to choose the lunch that matches his needs.

c/v 7 He sent the invoice covering the victory convention to Vick.

d/e 8 Edward decided that the deal with Deborah led to a dead end.

d/k 9 Dick and Kendra picked me up at the dock where I was parked.

e/i 10 Neither Erin nor Eric entertained their neighbors that time.

e/t 11 The time they established to meet us there was their choice.

e/x 12 The experts expect the Texan to explain the extra two texts.

f/d 13 Fred and my friends offered to defer the federal food funds.

f/g 14 Gifford was flying their flag but was frightened by the fog.

f/r 15 Francis is my freshman friend who first referred Fred to me.

g/b 16 My neighbor bragged when he brought the bags to the Egberts.

g/h 17 Although Hugh was frightened, he sought help from neighbors.

g/t 18 Together, Gretta and Agatha brought their gifts to the gate.

i/k 19 Katrina disliked the khaki skirts but liked the kilt design.

i/n 20 Orrin insinuated that Nina Knight might be in India tonight.

i/u 21 The university rebuilt the building using the unified units.

j/h 22 Jay has a jellyfish whose height is half the jeweler's junk.

j/k 23 As her jockey joked with my team, Jake jerked at his jacket.

k/l 24 Likewise, Kelvin Nickle disliked the kiln that Kilmer built.

Continued

© by the Glencoe Division of Macmillan/McGraw-Hill.

NAME DATE CLASS

Accuracy Practice Continued

SS or default

SM: Default or 1″

These sentences contain letter combinations that are either common in keyboarding or are difficult to key.

Practice those sentences containing letter combinations that you find troublesome.

Key each line at a comfortable pace. If you make an error, start again, keying more slowly. Stay on a line until you have keyed it without error.

m/n 25 Many of the memos were meant for our men and women managers.

n/d 26 Indeed, we found the kind of friends who wouldn't hinder us.

o/i 27 Point out my opinion that Union Oil has a joint oil venture.

o/l 28 Lorna looked lonely when the old location was sold to Golda.

o/r 29 Ronald ordered the organs from the North Orient Organ Group.

p/o 30 We hope to have the opportunity to pose an opposite opinion.

q/a 31 I quarrel about the quarterly quality and quantity outcomes.

q/u 32 We acquired quite a few aqua quilts quietly and yet quickly.

q/w 33 Que worked quietly on the quiz show quite often on weekends.

r/e 34 Red Redford was ready to return her share of their earnings.

r/t 35 Troy tried to travel entirely via train throughout the trip.

r/u 36 During the reunion, Ruth urged the juniors to set the rules.

s/c 37 The school for scuba diving is scheduled at Scorpius School.

s/d 38 Syd said he is sad that I sold my second saddle on Saturday.

s/e 39 Selma sent their senator several serious, searching queries.

s/h 40 Sheila wishes she had shipped Sherm's rush shipment herself.

s/t 41 The fast student keyboarder startled their studious visitor.

s/w 42 The Swimming Swede did a swell swan dive at the Swanky Pool.

u/y 43 Assure your youth sunny July weather at the Yuma Youth Camp.

v/b 44 The fifteen benevolent men had good vibes about the bivouac.

w/e 45 Wendy West welcomed the wet weather but wept at the wedding.

w/h 46 Those words are who, what, which, where, when, why, and how.

x/c/s 47 Cox Excavations executives had six excuses for excise taxes.

y/t 48 Today, the youths have not yet keyed what they typically do.

z/a 49 Zane is amazingly zealous about his Lazy Z Ranch in Arizona.

© by the Glencoe Division of Macmillan/McGraw-Hill.

NAME DATE CLASS

Language Arts ACTIVITY 2

Read the rules at the right. Then apply them to the practice words given. Refer to a dictionary if necessary.

Word Division Rules (Use with Lesson 39C)

Rule 4 Avoid dividing figures, abbreviations, dates, or proper nouns.
Rule 5 Divide a compound word between the elements or at the point of the hyphen.

Examples:

Word	Syllables	Divided Word	Rule Number
$76,982	-------	avoid dividing	4
blackboard	black board	black-board	5
Sarah Kline	-------	avoid dividing	4

Practice:

1. self-denial
2. March 17, 1990
3. $509,831
4. Joe Duggan, Ph.D.
5. outfield

Continued

© by the Glencoe Division of Macmillan/McGraw-Hill.

NAME DATE CLASS

Language Arts ACTIVITY 1

Read the rules at the right. Then apply them to the practice words given. Refer to a dictionary if necessary.

Word Division Rules (Use with Lesson 38C)

Rule 1 Never divide a one-syllable word or one with five or fewer letters.
Rule 2 Divide only between syllables.
Rule 3 Include two or more letters with the first part of the divided word and three or more with the last part.

Examples:

Word	Syllables	Divided Word	Rule Number
about	a bout	do not divide	1
sitter	sit ter	sit-ter	2
aquarium	a quar i um	aquar-ium	3

Practice:

1. litigant
2. permanent
3. imperialism
4. month
5. identity

Continued

© by the Glencoe Division of Macmillan/McGraw-Hill.

NAME DATE CLASS

Language Arts ACTIVITY 2 Continued

Circle the 12 words that have been divided incorrectly in the paragraph at the right. In the spaces provided, correctly divide those words.

Place the number of the word division rule that applies from page 19 after the word.

The National Association of Young Writers is presen-
tly planning to hold its annual conference in San Fr-
ancisco, California, next September. Arrangements mu-
st be made for tours of the city for all guests on the-
ir first day. A morning bus tour would be just perf-
ect. Then, for the participants' first free aftern-
oon in San Francisco, a trip to the Bank of Californi-
a's Collection of Money or to Chinatown would be intri-
guing. Their second full day should be spent at Fishe-
rman's Wharf, California's major tourist attraction.
All the young writers should be told of the famous sou-
rdough bread and should try to buy some. No trip to "S.-
F." would be complete without a visit to the Golden Ga-
te Bridge.

1. ______________
2. ______________
3. ______________
4. ______________
5. ______________
6. ______________
7. ______________
8. ______________
9. ______________
10. ______________
11. ______________
12. ______________

© by the Glencoe Division of Macmillan/McGraw-Hill.

NAME DATE CLASS

Language Arts ACTIVITY 1 Continued

The words at the right are divided incorrectly. Divide them correctly in the space provided, and write the number of the word division rule from page 19 that applies. Refer to a dictionary if necessary.

Word	Correct Division	Rule
1. miss-pelled		
2. barg-ain		
3. u-pon		
4. pract-ice		
5. en-cyclopedia		
6. ch-air		
7. ov-en		
8. gall-ery		
9. fol-der		
10. live-ry		
11. ex-cellent		
12. potassi-um		

© by the Glencoe Division of Macmillan/McGraw-Hill.

NAME DATE CLASS

Language Arts ACTIVITY 4

Read the rules at the right. Then apply the rules to the practice sentences given.

Capitalization Rules (Use with Lessons 41B and 43D)

Capitalize days of the week, months of the year, and holidays.

Capitalize all important words in business names, names of organizations, institutions, schools, and clubs. Refer to the organization's letterhead for the preferred capitalization. Do not capitalize *the, and,* and *of* and other such words unless they are the first word of the business name.

Examples:

We are taking our vacation the week of Memorial Day.
She always orders flower arrangements from The Red Rose.

Practice:

1. The conference runs from monday, august 1, to friday, august 5.
2. maple tree nursery offers a large selection of trees and shrubs.
3. Robert asked true typewriters, inc., to repair all the typewriters.
4. The labor day holiday is the first monday in september.
5. Agatha bought her book in a store named the book port.

Continued

© by the Glencoe Division of Macmillan/McGraw-Hill.

NAME DATE CLASS

Language Arts ACTIVITY 3

Read the rules at the right. Then underscore the common nouns and circle the proper nouns.

Capitalization Rules (Use with Lessons 20D and 24E)

A common noun names a person, place, thing, or idea in a general class. A common noun is not capitalized unless it begins a sentence.

Capitalize proper nouns. A proper noun names a specific person, place, or thing.

Examples:

The flowers in the garden are growing very fast.
The MacKenzies want to order a new Rabbit computer.

Practice:

1. Would you please pick up two zucchini at Johnsons' Farm?
2. There is a special sale at Clarke's Department Store today.
3. We need to order two new typewriters and two printers.
4. Paul Roberts and Louise Cohen will be married in Toledo.
5. Our company has changed its name to Cohen and Bornstein, Inc.

Continued

© by the Glencoe Division of Macmillan/McGraw-Hill.

NAME DATE CLASS

Language Arts ACTIVITY 4 Continued

Read the paragraphs at the right. Find the nouns that are not capitalized correctly and circle them. Key the paragraphs correctly.

Beginning monday, october 2, the starlight construction company will be known as additions, etc. However, as of today, friday, august 14, all letters, memorandums, and other communications from starlight construction company should show the new name, additions, etc. The name change was necessitated because of too much confusion between this company and starline construction company.

We will need to let all our customers know of the name change; therefore, please call franklin press and o. j. printing on monday to obtain estimates for printing name change cards. We will need them immediately after labor day, monday, september 4. If neither company would be able to have the cards ready by september 4, then let me know, and I will call quick print, inc. Quick print can usually have orders ready within one month.

© by the Glencoe Division of Macmillan/McGraw-Hill.

NAME DATE CLASS

Language Arts ACTIVITY 3 Continued

Circle the errors in capitalization in the sentences at the right. Then key the sentences using correct capitalization.

1. Ms. mary johnson just opened a store in San Diego, california.
2. The company needs to order ten new zebra cars this month.
3. juan sent peter to buy eight new ribbons at Computers, Inc.
4. These Documents must reach 110 shoreline drive by 3 p.m.
5. Please write the name of the Business on this note card.
6. clients from 32 States will be present at the meeting.
7. Have you ever used the fox computer and printer?
8. Did you send the Reports to Speedy Printer or Zip Print for Copies?
9. How many books by roberto dardino have you read?
10. Mrs. gravina made reservations for eight for the shea and golden familes.
11. Whom do you call when repairs are needed on the toby 1000?
12. Did juanita receive the package her Aunt cecelia jones sent?
13. all Tickets purchased through Year-Round Travel need to be returned for Refunds.
14. With the addition of two new Staff people, we will need two new Desks and Computers.
15. When are ms. jennings and mr. allin expected to arrive?

© by the Glencoe Division of Macmillan/McGraw-Hill.

NAME DATE CLASS

Language Arts ACTIVITY 6

Read the definitions at the right. Then use the correct form of the word in the practice sentences given.

Confusing Words (Use with Lessons 57E, 58C, and 59C)

their	Possessive form of *they*
there	In that place; opposite of *here*
they're	Contraction for *they are*
your	Possessive form of *you*
you're	Contraction for *you are*
are	Present tense form of the verb *be*
hour	60 minutes
our	Possessive form of *we*

Examples:

Please have the children put <u>their</u> toys over <u>there</u>.
<u>They're</u> in the process of renovating <u>your</u> house, aren't they?

Practice:

1. Do the managers have all _______ materials for the one _______ meeting?
2. If you and John _______ sure of _______ speeds, you may record them.
3. We need _______ materials over _______ before 2 p.m.

Continued

© by the Glencoe Division of Macmillan/McGraw-Hill.

NAME DATE CLASS

Language Arts ACTIVITY 5

Read the definitions at the right. Then use the correct word in the practice sentences given.

Confusing Words (Use with Lessons 51B and 55C)

it's	Contraction of *it is* and *it has*
its	Possessive form of the pronoun *it*
to	In the direction of (preposition)
too	In addition; excessively (adverb)
two	One more than one (noun or adjective)

Examples:

<u>It's</u> been months since the suitcase broke, and I have not fixed <u>its</u> lock.
They will need <u>two</u> printers and five computers, <u>too</u>.

Practice:

1. Pioneer, Inc. is sending _______ of _______ clients _______ Bermuda.
2. _______ been _______ long since we have seen each other.
3. Have you heard whether the second contract was approved, _______?
4. Do you know how long _______ been since the dog has had _______ hair brushed?
5. The company will send _______ employees _______ the regional meeting.

Continued

© by the Glencoe Division of Macmillan/McGraw-Hill.

NAME ____________ DATE ____________ CLASS ____________

Language Arts ACTIVITY 6 Continued

In the paragraph at the right, some words have been used incorrectly. Circle them, and then write the correct form on the lines provided.

The O'Connors have hired College Pro Painters to paint there house. Although their a young company, they hour well known. It generally takes them 28 ours to paint a house the size of yours. The O'Connors' house, though, would probably take much longer. They're our other painting companies available, but your never sure of the quality of work your getting unless you see there work. Hour house needs to be painted, too. Next time that you our going over their, please ask one of the painters to call me. I think that there just great. Please tell them we hour in no rush, but we would like to see there price list as soon as possible.

1. ____________
2. ____________
3. ____________
4. ____________
5. ____________
6. ____________
7. ____________
8. ____________
9. ____________
10. ____________
11. ____________
12. ____________
13. ____________
14. ____________
15. ____________

© by the Glencoe Division of Macmillan/McGraw-Hill.

NAME ____________ DATE ____________ CLASS ____________

Language Arts ACTIVITY 5 Continued

In the paragraph at the right, blank spaces have been left where a word is needed.

Supply the correct word from those on page 23. Then key the paragraph.

The sales managers have decided that ____________ a good idea to offer new bonuses this year, ____________. Each sales representative is already eligible for the company's stock and ____________ pension plan. The bonuses will be awarded ____________ those who increase their sales substantially over last year's sales. The company will now offer bonuses ____________ all ____________ sales representatives, not just ____________ ____________ top representatives. This policy will allow the ____________ newer employees a chance to earn more money, ____________. ____________ never ____________ soon ____________ try to earn a bonus! The company has decided ____________ award the bonuses to those receiving them during the last ____________ weeks of the year. We are all sure that ____________ going to be quite an incentive to try ____________ sell, sell, sell this year.

© by the Glencoe Division of Macmillan/McGraw-Hill.

NAME DATE CLASS

Language Arts REVIEW 1 (Use after Lesson 67C)

The sentences at the right are a review of all the rules presented in Language Arts.

Circle the errors as you find them. Then key the sentences, correcting the errors you found.

1. This year's seminar for (your/you're) team will meet on monday, january 25.
2. His latest poem, A Summer's Day, will be among several poems read on Channel 2's series, Young Writers.
3. Can you help solve (their/there/they're) computer problems, (to/too/two)?
4. (Are/Hour/Our) last meeting will be a 5 p.m. at the garden restaurant.
5. Before buying a Bicycle, check (to/too/two) see whether (your/you're) really getting the one that you want.
6. When are you moving to (your/you're) new apartment? asked Margaret.
7. Katie wrote Computers in Schools, which appeared in her local newspaper, the norfolk gazette.
8. The Accounting Department needs ten new Typewriters before memorial day.
9. Children are allowed to use (their/there/they're) computers if (are/hour/our) supervisors are available.
10. Please bring the Report to me by wednesday, july 17.

© by the Glencoe Division of Macmillan/McGraw-Hill.

NAME DATE CLASS

Language Arts ACTIVITY 7

Read the rules at the right. Then apply them to the practice sentences given.

Punctuation Rules (Use with Lessons 61C, 63C, and 67C)

Place quotation marks around the titles of articles, speeches, book chapters, songs, poems, and titles of episodes in a television series.

Underscore titles of books, magazines, newspapers, movies, plays, and television series. Underscore all words, spaces, and punctuation marks that are part of the title itself. In printed material, these titles are shown in italics (not underscored).

Use quotation marks to set off a direct quotation (a person's exact words).

Examples:

Mr. Jones wrote "Writing in Spanish" for <u>The Writer's Guide</u>.
Our office receives <u>The Daily Journal</u> and <u>Office Automation</u>.
"When do you think the conference will be over?" asked Mr. Gould.

Practice:

1. Franklin Peters will deliver his speech, Learning Is Easy, on Tuesday.
2. Have you seen the first part of the television series, The Human Brain?
3. Would you be able, she asked, to make my plane reservations?

Continued

© by the Glencoe Division of Macmillan/McGraw-Hill.

NAME DATE CLASS

Language Arts REVIEW 2 (Use after Lesson 67C)

The paragraph at the right is a review of all the rules presented in Language Arts.

Circle the errors as you find them. Then key the paragraph, correcting the errors you found.

The Library is a wonderful resource that is underused. Its very often overlooked by to many people. Almost every Town has a library, and its available to everyone. Hour you using you're library to it's fullest? They're are many resources in it. Books and Magazines are available at you're library, as well as local newspapers, such as The Milton Daily. If you asked you're Librarian, Please help me find the book Iguanas in St. Thomas, he or she could probably help you find it. Most Libraries are open monday through saturday, except for Holidays, such as memorial day and thanksgiving.

Libraries can help you when your looking for a job. Books such as The Occupational Outlook Handbook can help you discover what you might like to do and what sort of future you would find in various fields. Also, most libraries keep some Annual Reports from a number of companies. Its to easy too overlook you're Library. Librarians unite in saying, Please use you're library.

© by the Glencoe Division of Macmillan/McGraw-Hill.

NAME DATE CLASS

Language Arts ACTIVITY 7 Continued

In the paragraph at the right, supply underscores and quotation marks as needed.

After the disaster we had last year at the fall conference, Mr. Clarke began, we will be better prepared this year for our fall sales conference. Mrs. Smith agreed and suggested that everyone attending the conference read Windows on the World, which appeared in the July issue of Window Magic. Ms. Kelly remarked, The Chicago Daily and Architectural Advantages are highly recommended reading. Building Your Own Home, which is a television series on Channel 11 every Saturday afternoon, would also be helpful for everyone to watch. Mr. Clarke questioned whether anyone had read Mrs. Burrow's article, Windows: The Allure of the Outdoors or seen the movie, Opening Up Your Home? Although no one had either read the article or seen the movie, most of the people present said that they would try to do one or the other. All the sales representatives and sales managers present agreed to be better prepared for the fall conference; and to prove it, they all started singing the company song, Windows Are Better Than Doors to the World Outdoors.

© by the Glencoe Division of Macmillan/McGraw-Hill.

NAME DATE CLASS

Review UNIT 1: Alphabetic Keys

Indicate by circling T or F whether each statement at the right is true or false.

True or False

ANSWERS

1. Proofreading, or finding misstrokes, is as important as keying accurately. 1. T F
2. Good keystroking technique includes keeping your wrists low and almost motionless. 2. T F
3. Keeping your fingers straight when keying gives them power. 3. T F
4. When keying, you should pause between words to make sure that you have not made any misstrokes. 4. T F
5. The abbreviation for gross words a minute is GWAM. 5. T F
6. To determine your GWAM, begin by counting all lines keyed—complete and incomplete. 6. T F
7. When proofreading, treat errors in spacing and in punctuation following words as separate misstrokes. 7. T F
8. To stay comfortable, you may rest your hands on the frame of your keyboard as you key. 8. T F
9. The tab moves the carrier/cursor directly to a tab stop. 9. T F
10. On a 10-pitch typewriter, your margins would be set on 20 and 80 for side margins of 1″. 10. T F
11. When inserting paper, feed the paper into the machine by using the automatic paper insert or by turning the platen knob. 11. T F

M 10. When loading a disk, insert the program disk into Drive 1 and the student disk into Drive 2. 10. T F

11. A command is a message that appears on the display screen asking the user to respond. 11. T F

Select the word or phrase that best completes each statement at the right. Write the letter of the word or phrase in the Answers space.

Multiple Choice

1. Normally, you space (A) 1, (B) 2, (C) 3 time(s) between words. 1. ____
2. A line of text with 50 strokes has (A) 3 words, (B) 10 words, (C) 11 words. 2. ____
3. To indent for paragraphs, it is most efficient to use the (A) return/enter key, (B) space bar, (C) tab key. 3. ____
4. To leave two blank lines between text, you should (A) SS, (B) DS, (C) TS. 4. ____
5. If you keyed 75 words in 3 minutes, your GWAM would be (A) 25, (B) 30, (C) 50. 5. ____
6. The instructions (A) SM 1½″, (B) SS, (C) SM 2″ direct you to leave 1½-inch side margins. 6. ____
7. The 10-pitch type size has (A) 8, (B) 10, (C) 12 characters to a horizontal inch. 7. ____

© by the Glencoe Division of Macmillan/McGraw-Hill.

ANSWERS

8. When keying, rotate your wrists inward (A) not at all, (B) slightly, (C) quite a bit to position your fingers at right angles to the keys. 8. _____

9. Unless you are told otherwise, you should always leave about (A) ½ inch, (B) 1 inch, (C) 1½ inches at the top of your paper. 9. _____

10. To leave spaces between words and after marks of punctuation, use the (A) space bar, (B) tab key, (C) right shift key. 10. _____

11. If you set your line-space key/lever for double spacing, you will leave (A) one, (B) two, (C) three blank lines between text. 11. _____

12. To free a sheet of paper for removing or straightening, use the (A) paper guide, (B) page-end indicator, (C) paper release lever/bail. 12. _____

M 11. A disk that stores the data keyed by a student is called the (A) program disk, (B) student disk, (C) menu. 11. _____

12. The default setting for line spacing is usually (A) single, (B) double, (C) triple spacing. 12. _____

Completion

Complete each statement at the right by writing the correct word, number, or phrase in the blank.

1. Space _______ after a period used with an initial or an abbreviation.
2. When keying in 12 pitch, the settings for 1½″ side margins are _______ and _______.
3. In keyboarding, every _______ stroke(s) count(s) as one "word."
4. Use the __________________ finger to operate the return/enter key.
5. The __________________ thumb is used to operate the space bar.
6. If you keyed a total of 135 strokes, you keyed _______ words.
7. When keying in 12 pitch, the settings for 2″ side margins are _______ and _______.
8. The 12-pitch type size has _______ characters to a horizontal inch.
9. In home-key position, the right hand covers the __________________ keys.
10. In home-key position, the left hand covers the __________________ keys.
11. To set a 12-space tab indent, space over _______ spaces and press the appropriate key or command.
12. For most documents, align the paper guide at __________________.

© by the Glencoe Division of Macmillan/McGraw-Hill.

NAME DATE CLASS

Keyboard Composition

SS or default

SM: Default or 1″

Key each word at the right, followed by a colon. Then, key at least three words that rhyme with each word.

ACTIVITY 1 Use after Lesson 25D

1. face
2. mailing
3. clown
4. nice
5. taste
6. bowl
7. smile
8. date
9. look

Key a short answer for each question at the right.

ACTIVITY 2 Use after Lesson 26D

1. What is your first name?
2. What is your best friend's first name?
3. Is the weather sunny today?
4. Do you like to read books?
5. Would you rather work or play?
6. What is your favorite season of the year?

Key each sentence and the word that best completes it.

ACTIVITY 3 Use after Lesson 27E

1. A full sheet of paper has (6, 33, 66, 85) lines.
2. I am sitting at a (computer, typewriter).
3. My favorite season is (summer, fall, winter, spring).
4. I would rather (read, play sports, exercise).
5. My favorite yogurt flavor is (peach, strawberry, vanilla).
6. Of these, the fruit I like best is a(n) (apple, orange, pear).

Key each sentence, completing it with a one-word answer.

ACTIVITY 4 Use after Lesson 28D

1. The sport I like to watch is . . .
2. I was born in the city and state of . . .
3. My keyboarding teacher's full name is . . .
4. The food I like best is . . .
5. The music I like best is . . .

Answer each question with a short answer.

ACTIVITY 5 Use after Lesson 29E

1. What is your street address?
2. In what location do you usually study?
3. In what two ways do you plan to use your keyboarding skills?
4. What courses are you taking this term?
5. What is the complete name of your school?

Key each sentence with the phrase that best completes it.

ACTIVITY 6 Use after Lesson 30F

1. I would like to spend my summer (in the mountains, in the city, at the beach).
2. This weekend, I might (read a book, see a movie, go to a party).
3. When I study, I must (have my radio on, have a quiet place, be at school) to get anything done.
4. I would rather work in a situation where I (worked alone, worked with one or two other people, worked with many people).
5. I would rather attend (a very big school, a very small school).

© by the Glencoe Division of Macmillan/McGraw-Hill.

Keyboard Composition Continued

SS or default

SM: Default or 1″

Key each sentence, completing it with a short phrase.

ACTIVITY 7 Use after Lesson 34D

1. On a rainy or snowy day, I like to . . .
2. I like to be with people who are . . .
3. In the fall, I like to . . .
4. I like music because . . .
5. I never seem to know where . . .
6. In tomorrow's world, there will be fewer . . .

Key each sentence, filling each blank with a word or a short phrase.

ACTIVITY 8 Use after Lesson 37C

1. I have lived in ______ for ______ years.
2. In the morning, I get up at ______ and eat ______ for breakfast.
3. On Saturdays, I wake up at ______.
4. During my free time, I like to ______ outside.
5. I want a job that begins at ______ and ends at ______.
6. If I could earn double wages working overtime, I would ______.

Key the paragraph, filling each blank with a word or a short phrase or with one of the choices offered.

ACTIVITY 9 Use after Lesson 43B

I was born in the city of ______ in ______. I have ______ brothers and ______ sisters. I live in (a house, a condominium, an apartment) about ______ from school. My favorite room at home is ______. When I want to listen to my stereo, I go to ______. I (am, am not) responsible for taking care of tasks around the home, like ______. I (do, do not) receive an allowance to take care of (all, part of) my expenses. I do a (good job, fair job, poor job) of budgeting my money.

Answer each question with a complete sentence.

ACTIVITY 10 Use after Lesson 45D

1. Name three jobs in which a keyboarding skill is important.
2. Name other classes where your keyboarding skills will help you.
3. What did you eat this morning for breakfast?
4. What do you like to eat in a typical lunch?
5. What is your favorite holiday?
6. What would you do if you didn't understand material covered in class?

Use each of the words or phrases listed at the right in a complete sentence.

ACTIVITY 11 Use after Lessons 50C and 53B

bicycle	letter writing	next trip
magazine	winter	playing tennis
my future	birthdays	reports

© by the Glencoe Division of Macmillan/McGraw-Hill.

Keyboard Composition Continued

Read the information at the right. Then continue with the composing activities on Page 32.

ACTIVITY 12 Use before Lesson 57

When you are asked to complete a topic sentence, answer a question, or compose two paragraphs, you need to think about your response and then organize it. Planning will help you to compose quickly and efficiently. Below are two examples of typical composing activities. Follow the planning process closely.

Topics:

1. My favorite season is ______ because . . .
2. Write two paragraphs describing what a typical day is for you.

Step 1: Make a list of all the ideas or words that you can think of related to the topic. Write them down as quickly as possible. Don't try to sort them out. This step is called *brainstorming.*

Sample Lists:

Topic 1: My Favorite Season

summer
warm
swimming
hiking
no school
sailing
ice cream
vacation
sleep late

Topic 2: A Typical Day

school
feed the cat
breakfast
dinner
basketball
homework
paper route
walk the dog

Step 2: Once you finish brainstorming, find an order to your list. For example, in the list for Topic 1, you could group all your favorite activities and write about them first. Then, you could write about all the other fun parts to summer—for example, not having to go to school and being able to sleep late. A sample paragraph for Topic 1 follows.

My favorite season is summer because I enjoy summer activities. I like to go hiking with my family and swimming with my friends. In August, my brother and I go to sailing camp, which is very challenging. Also, there is no school in the summer, so I can sleep late if I want. When I finally do get up, there is always plenty of ice cream.

For any writing assignment, it is important to plan what you want to say. Planning is especially important when you compose at the keyboard. Thinking about what you will say and how you will say it *before* you actually begin to write will result in a clearer, more organized response. No matter what you are asked to write, you will find it easier to compose if you follow this two-step planning process.

Now it is your turn to try composing a paragraph for Topic 2: A Typical Day. Find an order for this list that is comfortable to you. You may add to the list if you like. Then compose the paragraph at the keyboard.

© by the Glencoe Division of Macmillan/McGraw-Hill.

Keyboard Composition Continued

Read the information at the right. Then apply what you have learned in the activities that follow.

For the activities that follow, try brainstorming before you begin composing at the keyboard. Once you have two lists from which to choose, pick the list that you think will help you write the more informative and interesting answer.

For activities 13 and 14, choose one of the two sentences at the right to complete. Use it as the beginning of a short paragraph.

ACTIVITY 13 Use after Lessons 57F and 58E

1. I like to read ______ books because . . .
2. My family is going to visit ______ because . . .

ACTIVITY 14 Use after Lesson 61D

1. If I could build anything in the world, I would build ______ because . . .
2. If I could live anywhere in the world, I would choose ______ because . . .

For activity 15, choose one of the two questions at the right. Use your answer to it as the beginning of a paragraph.

ACTIVITY 15 Use after Lesson 64C

1. What job have you heard about recently that sounds interesting?
2. What is your favorite animal and why?

For activity 16, choose one of the two topics at the right, and write two paragraphs about it.

ACTIVITY 16 Use after Lesson 68C

1. Write two paragraphs describing your neighborhood.
2. Write two paragraphs about your favorite way to travel.

© by the Glencoe Division of Macmillan/McGraw-Hill.

NAME DATE CLASS

Review UNIT 2: Number and Symbol Keys

Indicate by circling T or F whether each statement at the right is true or false.

True or False

ANSWERS

1. Leave a space between a quotation mark and the first letter of the word being quoted. **1.** T F
2. Space twice after a period that ends a sentence except at the end of a line of text. **2.** T F
3. Do not space before or after the diagonal in a fraction. **3.** T F
4. Space twice after a period used as a decimal. **4.** T F
5. You should always space twice after a colon used to express time. **5.** T F
6. GWAM means "gross words a minute." **6.** T F
7. Space once after a comma used to separate thousands and hundreds in numbers. **7.** T F
8. You should always space twice after a dash. **8.** T F
9. On most equipment, use the *sem* finger to strike the backspace key. **9.** T F
10. When editing text, you may insert, delete, rearrange, or correct errors. **10.** T F

M **10.** An embedded command, an instruction that is given to a computer, often does not appear on the display screen. **10.** T F

Select the word or phrase that best completes each statement at the right. Write the letter of the word or phrase in the Answers space.

Multiple Choice

1. In a hyphenated word, you should space (A) once, (B) twice, (C) not at all after the hyphen. **1.** _____
2. To key a series of letters in all capital letters, use the (A) shift key, (B) caps lock or shift lock key, (C) tab key. **2.** _____
3. The (A) colon, (B) quotation mark, (C) diagonal is used in made fractions. **3.** _____
4. A dash is made by keying (A) 1, (B) 2, (C) 3 hyphens. **4.** _____
5. Paragraphs are usually indented (A) 5, (B) 3, (C) 10 spaces. **5.** _____
6. The backspace key is usually operated with the (A) *a* finger, (B) *sem* finger, (C) *j* finger. **6.** _____
7. To find the number of words in a line of text, divide the number of strokes in the line by (A) the amount of time, (B) the number of misstrokes, (C) 5. **7.** _____
8. You should space (A) once, (B) twice, (C) not at all after a semicolon within a sentence. **8.** _____
9. To remove all tab stops, use the (A) tab clear key, (B) tab key, (C) return/enter key. **9.** _____

© by the Glencoe Division of Macmillan/McGraw-Hill.

10. The automatic return feature on electronic equipment is usually called (A) word wrap, (B) prompt, (C) return/enter key. 10. ____

M 10. Always remove a disk when the red light is (A) on, (B) off, (C) blinking. 10. ____

Complete each statement at the right by writing the correct word, number, or phrase in the blank.

Completion

1. The ________________ keys letters or words in all capitals.
2. The ________________ key permits you to move back one space at a time.
3. The question mark is usually keyed with the ________________ finger.
4. Space ______ time(s) after a colon used as a mark of punctuation.
5. Space ______ time(s) after the diagonal in a fraction.
6. Space ______ time(s) between a number and a fraction.
7. If you keyed a total of 120 strokes, you have keyed ______ words.
8. A ________________ is made with two hyphens.
9. The backspace key is usually operated with the ________________ finger.
10. You should space ______ time(s) after a period at the end of a sentence (unless it occurs at the end of the text line).
11. You should space ______ time(s) after a colon used as a mark of punctuation within a sentence.
12. You should space ______ time(s) after a comma used to separate thousands and hundreds in numbers of four or more digits.
13. You should space ______ time(s) between the quotation marks and the text within them.
14. The number 8 is operated with the ________________ finger.

E M 13. The ________________ key is used with other keys to program the keyboard to carry out certain functions; for example, automatic centering.

14. As text is deleted, the remaining text will move ________________.

M 13. Use the ________________ to move through text on the display screen.

14. The ________________ is the most common storage medium that is used with microcomputers.

© by the Glencoe Division of Macmillan/McGraw-Hill.

NAME　　　DATE　　　CLASS

Proofreader's Marks

Mark and Meaning		Mark in Text	Corrected Text
^,	Insert a comma	Jane, Tom^, and Bill left.	Jane, Tom, and Bill left.
⊙	Insert a period	Dr⊙ Clay arrived at noon⊙	Dr. Clay arrived at noon.
lc or /	Lower case	He contacted A/C/E Moving Co.	He contacted Ace Moving Co.
⊐	Move right	My cousins will arrive on Friday ⊏or⊐ Saturday and leave Monday.	My cousins will arrive on Friday or Saturday and leave Monday.
⊏	Move left	Mr. Johnson said he would need ⊏ four 250-page notebooks.	Mr. Johnson said he would need four 250-page notebooks.
¶	Paragraph	¶ The stores will give a 10 per-cent discount on Friday.	The stores will give a 10 percent discount on Friday.
stet	Let it stand; ignore correction	Carol Alridge has been a ~~close~~ (stet) friend of mine for five years.	Carol Alridge has been a close friend of mine for five years.

© by the Glencoe Division of Macmillan/McGraw-Hill.

NAME　　　DATE　　　CLASS

Proofreader's Marks

Proofreader's marks are used to correct or change printed or keyed copy. A person must be able to interpret these marks correctly when keying or rekeying the rough draft (corrected) copy. This table shows the most commonly used proofreader's marks, how they would appear on the rough draft, and how the rough draft copy would be correctly keyed.

Mark and Meaning		Mark in Text	Corrected Text
^	Insert	Come to ^(the) May 3 convention.	Come to the May 3 convention.
℘	Delete	He will sign ~~sign~~ the letter.	He will sign the letter.
#	Add space	We are#not going away.	We are not going away.
⁀	Close up space	Don't delay; do it to⁀day.	Don't delay; do it today.
≡	Capitalize	Rick attends boston college.	Rick attends Boston College.
∽	Change the order	We hoep to then see you.	We hope to see you then.

© by the Glencoe Division of Macmillan/McGraw-Hill.

NAME DATE CLASS

Proofreading Practice ACTIVITY 2

The first sentence in each pair at the right is keyed correctly. Compare the second sentence with the first, and use proofreader's marks to correct any error(s) you find.

1. Who will be the next famous guest speaker for you?
   Who will be the nxt famout guest speakre for you?
2. Are there computers here that I could use Tuesday?
   Are their Computers here tht I could use Teusday?
3. The books must be balanced by the end of the week.
   The boks mustbe ballanced by the end of this week
4. Kay keyed one letter, five memos, and six reports.
   Kay keyed on letter five memos and six repotrs.
5. Learning to write is not as difficult as it seems.
   Learning write to is not as difficult sa it seems.
6. The bill for the paper for $54.69 is due March 17.
   The bil for the paper for $4569 is do March 17.

© by the Glencoe Division of Macmillan/McGraw-Hill.

NAME DATE CLASS

Proofreading Practice ACTIVITY 1

The first sentence in each pair at the right is keyed correctly. Compare the second sentence with the first, and use proofreader's marks to correct any error(s) you find.

1. He needs $1,401,750 for this year's salary raises.
   He need $1,401,705 for this years' salary raises.
2. Have you submitted your entry for the poetry fair?
   Have you submited your entre for the poetry fair?
3. Please finish the order today. It must be mailed.
   Please finish teh order today. it must be mailed.
4. Did you apply for the position at the new company?
   Hid you apply for the postiion at the new comapny?
5. Professor Duhamel will speak to the class Tuesday.
   Professro duhamle will speek to the class Teusday.
6. Do all of you have dictionaries readily available?
   Doall fo you have dictionries readdily available?

© by the Glencoe Division of Macmillan/McGraw-Hill.

NAME DATE CLASS

Proofreading Practice ACTIVITY 5

Compare the keyed table with the handwritten one. Use proofreader's marks to indicate any corrections that must be made in the keyed version. Then key the table.

SALES FIGURES

Salesperson	1988	1989
D. Pickering	$37,089	$39,422
M. Coles	29,614	31,200
K. Wu	34,102	38,500
T. Bohorquez	41,786	42,999

Sale Figures

Salesperson	1988	1999
D. Pickerign	$37,089	$39,422
M. Cole	29,641	31,200
K. Wu	34,102	35,800
T. Bohorquz	41,768	42,999

© by the Glencoe Division of Macmillan/McGraw-Hill.

NAME DATE CLASS

Proofreading Practice ACTIVITY 3

Compare the names in Column 1 with those in Column 2. Place a check mark in the appropriate column to indicate whether they are alike or not alike.

COLUMN 1	COLUMN 2		Alike	Not Alike
Ms. B. C. Roberts	Ms. B. R. Roberts	1.	_____	_____
Ruth Davis	Ruth Davis	2.	_____	_____
T. E. McDonough & Co.	T. E. MacDonough & Co.	3.	_____	_____
Lisa Kasprzak	Lisa R. Kasprzak	4.	_____	_____
The Enchanted Florist	The Enchanted Forest	5.	_____	_____
Mrs. W. Blake Coles	Mrs. W. Blak Coles	6.	_____	_____
Dr. Anne Schintzius	Dr. Ann Schintzius	7.	_____	_____
Maria Parker-Goulding	Maria Parker Goulding	8.	_____	_____
Mr. Franklin T. Leave	Mr. Franklin T. Leave	9.	_____	_____
Mrs. Peter Wu	Ms. Peter Wu	10.	_____	_____

© by the Glencoe Division of Macmillan/McGraw-Hill.

NAME DATE CLASS

Proofreading Practice ACTIVITY 6

Proofread the paragraphs at the right. Use proofreader's marks to indicate any corrections that need to be made. Then key the corrected paragraph.

There si no need to to be a "wallflower" when your in agroup. You cna be-come part if teh conversaition with out bein over-bearing. If you you are het type of persons who say nothing in group situation, it's easy easy to over come thes hangup. Ina wordd, it's <u>Enthusiiasm</u>. when you are a in converversation, shiftp your thinkin in to hegh gear and git excitedd about whatt's beeing discusssed.. Than you'll auto-mmatically speek yp adn be abl to ad to the the converasation.

Fearr is comon whin you're innolved in a conversation.The easiest way too rise above faer si to steer you thinkingaway from yourr ffears. As your thinking veccomes moore pospositive dna consturctive, your pirsonallity wil automaticaly takeon a new tonne.

© by the Glencoe Division of Macmillan/McGraw-Hill.

NAME DATE CLASS

Proofreading Practice ACTIVITY 4

Compare the numbers in Columns A, B, and C with those in Column 1. Indicate which, if any, of the numbers do *not* match those in Column 1 by writing the letter or letters of the incorrect column(s) in the Answers space. If all columns match the numbers in Column 1, write *all alike.*

COLUMN 1	COLUMN A	COLUMN B	COLUMN C	ANSWERS
6988074	6988074	6988047	6988074	1. ________
6/4/83	6/4/83	6/4/83	6/4/83	2. ________
BC-425	BC425	BC-425	CB-425	3. ________
14.679	14.769	14.679	14.679	4. ________
12 1/2	12 2/1	12 2/1	12 1/2	5. ________
2093221	2093212	2093221	2093221	6. ________
423H87	423H87	423H87	423H87	7. ________
9:31	9:31	9:13	9:13	8. ________
4998.08	4998.07	4998.08	499.808	9. ________
$13,765	$13,765	$13,765	$13,756	10. ________

© by the Glencoe Division of Macmillan/McGraw-Hill.

NAME DATE CLASS

Proofreading Practice ACTIVITY 7

Proofread the block format business letter at the right. Using proofreader's marks, indicate the corrections that need to be made. Then key the letter, making the necessary corrections.

November 17, 19--

Mr. Mark O'Leary
Offices, Incorporated
77 ParkSquare
New York, NY 10007

Dear Ms. O'Leary:

Your publicatoin called Office furniture is veery innforamative. Thanks yuo fro sendding it us to. i think that I will order our neew offiecdesks Form you

I would, however likee too seea sampel of the regal deks. Doo yo hvae of any theese Desks availeble for veiwing. I wwould be able to ex-amine thesse desks ayn monday tuesday or wednesday during the nxet few weks.

since We aer anxous to placceour ordre, pleaz calll me soon at 721-6790. I forward to heering form yoo.

Very Truley Yours

Meredith MacIntosh
purchising managre

© by the Glencoe Division of Macmillan/McGraw-Hill.

Proofreading Practice ACTIVITY 8

Proofread the block format business letter at the right. Using proofreader's marks, indicate the corrections that need to be made. Then rekey the letter, making the necessary corrections.

January 4, 19--

Ms. Rebecca Levy
H. T. Contstruction Compnay
4201 east street
Asn Francisco, CA 94188

Dear Ms. Levy,

The First phasse fo constructiontion on the medcial Lab looks excelllent. Every one seem thrilledwith teh nwe setup. is the completion datee february 17.

Becuase schedlling of, pleeae letus now the the Beginninng adn Endng dates fro the seecond phas by mondy, janyuary 11.

Wee have ben verry Pleasedwith your wokr, adn we antcipate uisng T. H. constructon agaiin in the futture.

Sincerly yours:

Roger cullen
Asistant Managager

© by the Glencoe Division of Macmillan/McGraw-Hill.

© by the Glencoe Division of Macmillan/McGraw-Hill.

The LINCOLN Company

437 Market Street
Providence, RI 02903
Phone (401) 388-9282

The LINCOLN Company

437 Market Street
Providence, RI 02903
Phone (401) 388-9282

HAUGEN & CATRON, Inc.

1304 Main Street
Montgomery, AL 36106

© by the Glencoe Division of Macmillan/McGraw-Hill.

Reliance Computer Co.

1414 West Armour Street
Chicago, IL 60624

© by the Glencoe Division of Macmillan/McGraw-Hill.

Aurora
Creative
Research,
Inc.

1107 Hibiscus Drive
Burnsville, SC 28714

© by the Glencoe Division of Macmillan/McGraw-Hill.

CB PRODUCTS
511 Walnut Street, Cincinnati, Ohio 45202

© by the Glencoe Division of Macmillan/McGraw-Hill.

MARRON MANUFACTURING
700 First Avenue
Williamsport, PA 17701

MARRON MANUFACTURING
700 First Avenue
Williamsport, PA 17701

MARRON MANUFACTURING
700 First Avenue
Williamsport, PA 17701

MARRON MANUFACTURING
700 First Avenue
Williamsport, PA 17701

SYSTEMS COMPANY
414 East Walnut
Green Bay, WI 54301

© by the Glencoe Division of Macmillan/McGraw-Hill.

SYSTEMS COMPANY

414 East Walnut, Green Bay, WI 54301

Swanson, Worth & Beatty

877 Montrose Avenue, Warren, MI 48089

© by the Glencoe Division of Macmillan/McGraw-Hill.

Swanson, Worth & Beatty

877 Montrose Avenue, Warren, MI 48089

INDEPENDENT
RESEARCHERS, INC.
4200 FAIRHAVEN CIRCLE
DALLAS, TX 75234

© by the Glencoe Division of Macmillan/McGraw-Hill.

INDEPENDENT RESEARCHERS, INC.
4200 FAIRHAVEN CIRCLE
DALLAS, TX 75234

Bean & Dow, Inc.

5299 Brierwood Terrace,
Norwalk, CT 06850

© by the Glencoe Division of Macmillan/McGraw-Hill.

Bean & Dow, Inc.

5299 Brierwood Terrace, Norwalk, CT 06850   303-989-5839

Enrichment Opportunities: Letters

Key the letter at the right, using block format.

Send to:

Mr. Sheldon McDonnell
Manager
Data Information, Inc.
4390 Castle Rock Avenue
Hackensack, NJ 07606

From:

Marianne Chong
Sales Director

Date: Line 15

ACTIVITY 1

Nowadays, there are literally hundreds of different kinds of computers marketed by as many manufacturers. The complexity of each kind may vary considerably, but in the end, each computer has two fundamental sections--the control unit and the arithmetic and logic unit.

The control unit reads and interprets program instructions, directs the operation of internal processor components, and controls the flow of the programs and data in and out of primary storage. A program must first be loaded to primary storage before it can be executed.

The arithmetic and logic unit performs all computations (addition, subtraction, multiplication, and division) and all logic operations (comparisons). Examples of computations include the following: the payroll deduction for Social Security, the day-end inventory, and the balance on bank statements. A logic operation, on the other hand, is a comparison between two pieces of data. The arithmetic and logic unit also does alphabetic comparisons.

If you are interested in a further "look inside" the APPEX microcomputer, please join us on June 30 at 7 p.m. at The Hotel Hamlette.

Sincerely

© by the Glencoe Division of Macmillan/McGraw-Hill.

Enrichment Opportunities: Letters

Key the letter at the right, using block format.

Send to:

Mr. William Foster
421 Oak Street
Memphis, TN 38152

From:

Eunice Pearlman
Communications
Specialist

Date: Line 15

ACTIVITY 2

As you requested, I have gathered some

Bill, I hope this information will help you as you design your report on computers and communications. It seems computers are everywhere. However, we have only scratched the surfface fo possilbe computer aplaications. The outlook for innovative, exciting, and beneficial appications si very very promnising indeed.

Micro-miniaturization has away done with athe spaCE constraint and it has permitted the installation of computers in confined space. Tiny computers can now bre installed in charge cards. The distance constraint has been neutralized by Data Communications. You can access your computers just by using a tuoch telephone and template made to access the computers' functions.

Even the mail has been influenced by the computer. The traditional letter may never become obsolete, but electronic mail will become an an increasingly popular alternitive. To send an electronic letter an executive could dictate not to a secretary, but to a computer. The words would be transcribed directly into text, with out key entry.

The letter could then abe displayed on a Vdt or read by a a computer using synthesized speech. Good Luck with your report. I hope this helped.

Sincerely

© by the Glencoe Division of Macmillan/McGraw-Hill.

NAME DATE CLASS

Enrichment Opportunities: Letters Continued

The two block-format business letters at the right have formatting errors in them. Locate the errors, and write the correct formatting directions on the lines provided.

ACTIVITY 3

March 14, 19--

Ms. Jean Garvey
Manager
Baker Tools
15800 Pawnee Circle
Lincoln, NE 68506-6011
Dear Ms. Garvey

Business letters serve many important business functions, such as making sales, ordering products and services, informing customers, correcting problems, persuading buyers, making inquiries, and conveying goodwill.

Letters should make a favorable impression on those who receive them. Each letter should be arranged to be pleasing to the eye. It should be visually framed with approximately equal top and bottom margins.

Correspondence Specialist
Marcie Hobkirk

mao

1. ______
2. ______
3. ______
4. ______
5. ______

ACTIVITY 4

January 27, 19--

Mr. Michael L. Williams
Agent
Astro Travel, Inc.
13400 Ridgeway Road
Dallas, TX 75234

In response to your letter asking about the "rules of the air," I have compiled some information that may help you.

Federal law requires that all passengers who ask for seats in the nonsmoking section of the plane be given such seats. If the nonsmoking section is full, you must designate the first row in the smoking section as a nonsmoking area.

Another requirement is that all baggage must have the passenger's name clearly marked on the outside. Remind passengers to put their names inside their luggage and to carry all valuables (such as money, cameras, and jewelry) with them on board.

I will be happy to answer any other questions you might have about "rules of the air."

Sincerely

Antoinette Ninghetti
District Manager

1. ______
2. ______
3. ______
4. ______
5. ______

© by the Glencoe Division of Macmillan/McGraw-Hill.

Enrichment Opportunities: Letters Continued

Each address at the right is not in the correct order. Write each one in the correct order in the space provided.

ACTIVITY 5

Johnson Bank and Trust Company / Boise, ID 83707 / 149 East Main Street / Mr. John Kuppens / Senior Loan Officer

Ms. Barbara A. Jones / Boston, MA 02118 / Administrative Assistant / Barber Bros. / 5468 Lincoln Avenue

The Fabric Store, Inc. / New York, NY 10036 / 1200 West 44th Street / Mrs. Rose Doherty / Owner

ACTIVITY 6

Provide salutations for each of the addresses at the right. Use the space provided.

Mr. Ray Parker
Manager
Smith Construction
4201 Collamore Street
Hallowell, ME 04347

Mrs. Nancy Whitehead
Director of Marketing
DeTec, Inc.
807 Adams Street
Milton, MA 02186

Ms. Juanita Gomez
Assistant Superintendent
Mission Avenue Apartments
Ten Mission Avenue
Clearwater, FL 33519

Mr. Frank Bordeau
Special Agent
Fox Detective Agency
39 Detroit Avenue
Spokane, WA 99202

© by the Glencoe Division of Macmillan/McGraw-Hill.

NAME DATE CLASS

Review UNIT 3: Personal/Business Letters

Indicate by circling T or F whether each statement at the right is true or false.

True or False

ANSWERS

1. When ZIP-Plus is used, a hyphen and three figures follow the ZIP Code. 1. T F
2. The complimentary close is keyed a TS below the body of a letter. 2. T F
3. If a letter is addressed to a company, an appropriate salutation would be *Ladies and Gentlemen.* 3. T F
4. The proofreader's mark ⸍ means add space. 4. T F
5. *Very truly yours* is an example of a courtesy title. 5. T F
6. Personal business letters are usually keyed on letterhead stationery. 6. T F
7. It is proper to address a person by his or her first name in the salutation of a business letter. 7. T F
8. *Dear Mr. Kotson* is an example of a salutation. 8. T F
9. Business letters are usually keyed with side margins of 1″. 9. T F
10. When keying an envelope address in OCR format, you should omit all punctuation and key all letters as capital letters. 10. T F

M

9. When you store a document, you move it from the microcomputer's memory to a floppy disk. 9. T F
10. The print option or print command is used to retrieve a document. 10. T F

Select the word or phrase that best completes each statement at the right. Write the letter of the word or phrase in the Answers space.

Multiple Choice

1. In a business letter, the reference initials are those of the (A) originator, (B) keyboard operator, (C) addressee. 1. _____
2. In letters using the block format, all lines are keyed beginning at the (A) center, (B) right margin, (C) left margin. 2. _____
3. The originator of a letter is the person who (A) wrote the letter, (B) received the letter, (C) keyed the letter. 3. _____
4. Within the body of a letter, (A) SS, (B) DS, (C) TS between paragraphs. 4. _____
5. If you do not know the marital status of a woman, the correct courtesy title to use in a letter is (A) Ms., (B) Mrs., (C) Miss. 5. _____
6. The proofreader's mark ¶ means (A) move right, (B) new paragraph, (C) insert a period. 6. _____
7. To show that a comma must be inserted, you would mark your text with (A) ∧ , (B) ∧, , (C) # . 7. _____
8. When there is no colon after the salutation, the form of punctuation used is (A) mixed, (B) closed, (C) open. 8. _____

9. When keying an envelope address in OCR format, you should always leave a top margin of (A) 2", (B) 2 ½", (C) 3". 9. ____

10. When open punctuation is used in a letter, (A) a colon, (B) a comma, (C) no punctuation follows the salutation. 10. ____

E M 9. For line endings in the body of a letter, use the (A) return/enter key, (B) automatic word wrap, (C) tab key. 9. ____

10. If you have a default top margin of 6 lines, you should count down (A) 7, (B) 8, (C) 9 more lines to be on line 15 for the date line. 10. ____

Complete each statement at the right by writing the correct word, number, or phrase in the blank.

Completion

1. If you see the proofreader's mark ⊙ , it means ________________.
2. Leave a ________________ between the salutation and the inside address.
3. You can determine who keyed a letter by the ________________, keyed a double space below the signature lines.
4. When any changes or corrections need to be made in rough draft or keyed material, use the appropriate ________________.
5. The mailing address on the envelope should contain the same information that is in the ________________ of the letter.
6. Paragraphs of a business letter are generally ________________ spaced.
7. Key the mailing address on a No. 10 envelope ______ inches from the top of the envelope (approximately line 15).
8. If the first line of the inside address is Ms. Janet Sweet, an appropriate salutation would be ________________.
9. For business letters, the side margins for both the 10- and the 12-pitch type size should be ______ inch(es).
10. In the personal business letter, the address of the ________________ is keyed below the signature line.
11. The ________________ is the first part of a letter to be keyed.
12. If *self-addressed* appeared at the end of a line of text and needed to be divided, ________________ is how it should be divided. (Write *do not divide* if you should not divide the word.)
13. To indent for a paragraph, you should use the ________________.
14. If you do not have an automatic word wrap feature on your keyboard, you should use the ________________ at the end of lines of text to return the carrier/cursor.

E M 13. To enable the equipment to locate a document at a later date, give the document a ________________.

14. When you ________________ a document on electronic equipment, you are recalling a stored document.

© by the Glencoe Division of Macmillan/McGraw-Hill.

NAME DATE CLASS

Enrichment Opportunities: Centering

DS

Center the text in Activity 1 horizontally and vertically.

ACTIVITY 1

To take advantage of
special discounts
on high-quality brass beds
and other brass accessories,
attend the
GRAND OPENING
of
Far East Brass Imports
5599 Montview Boulevard
Wednesday, December 28, 19--
8 a.m. — 9 p.m.

DS

Center the text in Activity 2 horizontally and vertically.

ACTIVITY 2

The Psychology of ~~Winning~~ Success
~~Learn~~ Research the educational or experience requirements of your goals
write down ~~a few~~ specific, yet realistic long-term goals
Write down ~~some~~ daily or weekly short-term goals
Keep track of ~~all~~ your daily progress towards your goals
Keep a positive mental out look Your about future
Believe in your self ~~always~~
Be patient about your progress, yet keep the pace ~~very~~ steady

DS

Center the text in Activity 3 horizontally and vertically.

ACTIVITY 3

You are cordially invited to attend
the first public showing
of original watercolors
by
Pauline Marie Allin
The Wellesley College Club
Sunday, September 2, 19--
two to four o'clock
Reception in the Baker Room

© by the Glencoe Division of Macmillan/McGraw-Hill.

Enrichment Opportunities: Centering Continued

DS

Space between columns: 6

Center the text in Activity 4 horizontally and vertically.

ACTIVITY 4

SOME COLORADO HIGHLIGHTS AND LOCATIONS

Narrow Gauge Railway	Silverton, Durango
Longs Peak	Rocky Mountain National Park
Pikes Peak	Colorado Springs
Red Rocks Natural Amphitheater	Morrison
Royal Gorge Bridge and Park	Canon City
Glenwood Canyon	Glenwood Springs
Air Force Academy	Colorado Springs

DS

Space between columns: 8

Center the text in Activity 5 horizontally and vertically.

ACTIVITY 5

Fund Raising Events and Dollars Raised

Governor's Cup Marathon	$102,000
Mayor's 20K Run	75,000
Rocky Mountain Bike-A-Thon	43,500
Washington Park Fun-Run for Special Olympics	41,000
White River Forest Hike-A-Thon	28,000
Rabbit Ears Pass Race	8,900

DS

Space between columns: 8

Center the text in Activity 6 horizontally and vertically.

ACTIVITY 6

The Olympic Games

1968	Winter	Grenoble, France
1968	Summer	Mexico City
1972	Winter	Sapporo, Japan
1972	Summer	Munich
1976	Winter	Innsbruck, Austria
1976	Summer	Montreal
1980	Winter	Lake Placid
1980	Summer	Moscow
1984	Winter	Sarajevo, Yugoslavia
1984	Summer	Los Angeles
1988	Winter	Calgary, Alberta
1988	Summer	Seoul, South Korea

© by the Glencoe Division of Macmillan/McGraw-Hill.

NAME DATE CLASS

Enrichment Opportunities: Centering

Answer the questions that follow using the table at the right.

ACTIVITY 7

SPRING FLOWERING BULBS

Snowdrops	4"	March–April
Crocus	4½"	March–April
Jonquils	13"	March–April
Daffodils	18"	April–May
Hyacinths	10"	April–May
Fritillaria	23"	April–May
Lily-flowered Tulips	24"	May–June
Allium	10"	May–June

Answer questions 1–3 as though the table above were single-spaced using 10 pitch.

1. How many lines are used in this table? ________

2. What would the start line be for this table if vertically centered on a full sheet of paper? a half sheet? ________

3. What would the left and right margins be if this table were horizontally centered using 8 spaces between columns? ________

Answer questions 4–6 as though the table above were double-spaced using 12 pitch.

4. How many lines are used in this double-spaced table? ________

5. What would the start line be for this table if vertically centered on a full sheet of paper? a half sheet? ________

6. What would the margins and tab stops be for this table if horizontally centered on a full sheet of paper using 8 spaces between columns? ________

© by the Glencoe Division of Macmillan/McGraw-Hill.

NAME DATE CLASS

Enrichment Opportunities: Centering Continued

Based on the information given at the right, compute the start line for material that is to be centered vertically on a full sheet of paper.

ACTIVITY 8

1. Sixteen lines of text that are double spaced. ________
2. Twenty-four lines of text that are single spaced. ________
3. Twenty-four lines of text, double spaced. ________
4. Forty-three lines of text, single spaced. ________
5. Eighteen lines of text, double spaced. ________
6. Twenty-one lines of text, double spaced. ________
7. A title plus thirty-two lines of text that are single spaced. ________
8. A title plus forty lines of text that are single spaced. ________
9. A title plus ten lines of text that are double spaced. ________
10. A title plus twenty lines of text that are single spaced. ________
11. A title plus twenty-three lines of text that are double spaced. ________
12. A title plus fifty-one lines of text that are single spaced. ________

© by the Glencoe Division of Macmillan/McGraw-Hill.

NAME DATE CLASS

Review UNIT 4: Horizontal and Vertical Centering

Indicate by circling T or F whether each statement at the right is true or false.

True or False

ANSWERS

1. The title of a table should be keyed in capital and lower-case letters. 1. T F
2. When centering a document vertically, disregard fractions that remain after you divide by two. 2. T F
3. The center of a standard-size (8½″ × 11″) sheet of paper is 42 for 10 pitch. 3. T F
4. Three blank lines are left between the title and the body of the table. 4. T F
5. When you TS, 3 blank lines are left between the lines of text. 5. T F
6. To center a table vertically on a full sheet of paper, subtract the lines to be used from 66, divide by 2, and add 1. 6. T F
7. When keying material in three columns, you should begin the first column at the left margin. 7. T F
8. To prepare your equipment for keying columns of information, you should clear all tab stops. 8. T F
9. To center a title manually, backspace once for each character in the title, ignoring any single letter left over. 9. T F
10. In counting the lines of a double spaced table, ignore the blank lines between lines of text. 10. T F

E M 10. Automatic centering refers to a machine or software function that automatically centers words or lines horizontally. 10. T F

Select the word or phrase that best completes each statement at the right. Write the letter of the word or phrase in the Answers space.

Multiple Choice

1. To center a word horizontally, backspace from the center once for every (A) 2 letters or spaces, (B) 1 letter or space, (C) 3 letters or spaces. 1. ______
2. When you single space lines of text, you leave (A) 1, (B) 2, (C) 0 blank line(s) between the text lines. 2. ______
3. When keying tables, word columns should align on the (A) left, (B) right, (C) center point. 3. ______
4. To center vertically 32 single spaced lines of text, you would begin keying on (A) line 17, (B) line 18, (C) line 19. 4. ______
5. Before centering columns of text horizontally, (A) set 1″ SM, (B) clear all tab stops, (C) set the line-space lever at 2. 5. ______
6. To leave 3 blank lines between lines of text, (A) SS, (B) DS, (C) QS. 6. ______
7. When centering text vertically on a full sheet of paper, you subtract the number of lines used from (A) 66, (B) 33, (C) 12. 7. ______

© by the Glencoe Division of Macmillan/McGraw-Hill.

8. Before you begin keying columns, you should make sure your paper guide is set at (A) 0, (B) 10, (C) 12. 8. _____

9. If you are keying material in four columns, you should set a left margin and (A) 2, (B) 3, (C) 4 tab stops. 9. _____

10. The center point of a standard-size (8½" × 11") sheet of paper for 12 pitch is (A) 12, (B) 42, (C) 51. 10. _____

E M 9. When you are aligning columns of numbers containing decimals, use the (A) tab key, (B) decimal tab key, (C) space bar. 9. _____

10. When keying columns of numbers and using the decimal tab, you (A) always, (B) never, (C) sometimes determine the key line for the table. 10. _____

Completion

Complete each statement at the right by writing the correct word, number, or phrase in the blank.

1. The title of a table is ________________ and keyed in all capital letters.
2. When you SS, ______ blank line(s) is/are left between the keyed lines.
3. When centering columns horizontally, you should leave the same amount of space between the columns, usually ______ spaces.
4. When keying a column of numbers, the numbers should align at the ________________ or at the decimal point.
5. When you DS between text lines, ______ blank line(s) is/are left.
6. To center columns of words or numbers horizontally, begin by keying the ________________ line, which is made up of the longest word in each column and the spaces between the columns.
7. Columns that contain words should be aligned on the ________________.
8. To leave 10 blank lines for a top margin, begin keying on line ______.
9. When you backspace once for every two letters or spaces, ignoring any single letter left over, you are centering ________________.
10. When centering text vertically on a full sheet of paper, subtract the total number of lines used from ______.

E M 10. A machine or software function that automatically aligns columns of numbers at their decimal points is called ________________.

© by the Glencoe Division of Macmillan/McGraw-Hill.

NAME DATE CLASS

Enrichment Opportunities: Reports ACTIVITY 1

Key the report and the references in unbound report format.

FRUIT: AN ESSENTIAL ELEMENT IN YOUR DIET

The need for carbohydrates in the athlete's diet is legendary, but many people who exercise regularly forget that they, too, need carbohydrates. The good news, especially for people restricting their diets, is that carbohydrates are found in foods other than in pasta! Mother Nature has very cleverly combined carbohydrates, fiber, vitamins, minerals, and sweetness into an attractive item called fruit. A typical half-cup serving of fruit provides approximately 40 fat-free calories (Applegate 1987, 88).

Carbohydrates are just one of the essential elements in fruit. Fruits are an excellent source of vitamins and minerals. If you usually think only of fruits such as apples and oranges, expand your horizon and your diet to include some unusually tasty fruits. The yellow-orange flesh fruits--cantaloupes, persimmons, and papayas--provide us with beta-carotene, which is closely related to Vitamin A (Applegate 1987, 88). Vitamin C is found in the citrus fruits. In fact, a fruit that many people overlook, the kiwi fruit, contains 100 percent of the U. S. RDA (Recommended Daily Allowance) of Vitamin C. Best of all, the kiwi is low in fat; a single kiwi contains no more than 45 calories ("Kiwi Fruit Goes Mainstream" 1987, 90). All kinds of berries are also rich in Vitamin C.

Many dieticians recommend that you learn which of the dietary elements are in different fruits and that you eat two servings daily: one high in Vitamin A or beta-carotene and one high in Vitamin C.

Remember, the next time you need that quick burst of energy, reach for the natural source-- a fresh fruit.

REFERENCES

Applegate, Liz, Ph.D. 1987. Fabulous Fresh Fruit. Runner's World 22 (August): 88.

Kiwi Fruit Goes Mainstream. 1987. Better Homes and Gardens, 65(March): 90.

© by the Glencoe Division of Macmillan/McGraw-Hill.

NAME DATE CLASS

Enrichment Opportunities: Reports ACTIVITY 2

Key the report and the references at the right, using the unbound report format.

Make all the corrections indicated.

The title of the report is "Bring Your Own Computer?"

Who would have ever dreamt that the power of computer systems that filled an entire room would one day be reduced to a small unit designed to be completely portable? Who would would have ever dreamed that YOU would be able to atke your computer a board an airplane. Prior to 1984 many of the airlines baned the use fo lap top computers, believing that they interfered with the planes navigation and communication equipment. After the results of an faa study showed that they did not cause a problem a brand new day was bborn for business travelers (Antonoff 1987, 141).

Today these very popular computers caled lap tops ro portables are seen every day in airports, in meeting rooms, in hotel rooms and, of course, at home. sales greew bye 50 % in 1 recent year (Wallace 1987, 61).

Much of of the increase in slaes can be traced to an greatly improved product. The earliest lap top Computers ween limited edition: diskless, verry small displays and built-in soft ware that you had to use (Makrias 1987, 137). Those featurees have al improved been upon in todays models. Today's laptops include ten important features of running MS-DOS, using 3½-inch disks, and have larger, more readable screens and modems and printers on some models.

een with the adddition of new improved features, the typical business buyer si looking for some the of same basic features as the original models. It must bee compact and ti must be light. At the time same the developers are chalenged because the buyer reqwuires that perfformance not be sacrrificed for prtability (Unger 1987, 221). To date, they have been alhe to meet thyse demands. What s nexxt in the worlds of computers?

References

Antonoff, Michael. 1978. Airlines ZigZag On In Seat Computing. Personal Computing 10 (July): 141

Makiras, Stephen. 1987 Portable Computers. Personal Computing 11 (June): 137-8.

Ungre, John. 1987. Compaqs New Carry on. Byte 12 (May): 221.

wallace, John. 1987 Office in a Box. Working Women 12 (May): 60

© by the Glencoe Division of Macmillan/McGraw-Hill.

NAME DATE CLASS

Review UNIT 6: Unbound Reports

Indicate by circling T or F whether each statement at the right is true or false.

True or False

ANSWERS

1. An unbound report is usually long, and the pages are stapled or hole punched. 1. T F
2. The page number on a continuing page of an unbound report is keyed on line 7. 2. T F
3. The reference page lists the title of the report, the author's name, the date, and the name of the school. 3. T F
4. Long quotations are always indented 10 spaces from each margin. 4. T F
5. The bottom margin of all pages of unbound reports should be 2″. 5. T F
6. The top margin of page one of an unbound report is 2″. 6. T F
7. The entries on the reference page are listed in alphabetical order. 7. T F
8. The reference page uses the same side margins as the report. 8. T F
9. If your equipment allows you to key in 10 pitch or in 12 pitch, your margins remain the same when you change type size. 9. T F
10. The margin indicator/margin set keys control the beginning and ending of lines when you are keying an unbound report. 10. T F

E M 10. You should not include the default top margin when counting down to line 16 for the title page of a report. 10. T F

Select the word or phrase that best completes each statement at the right. Write the letter of the word or phrase in the Answers space.

Multiple Choice

1. Although there are several ways for a writer of a report to give credit for information taken from other sources and used in preparing the report, the author-date format is called (A) a footnote, (B) an endnote, (C) a parenthetical reference. 1. _____
2. A long quotation in the body of a report should be (A) indented 5 spaces from the left and right margins, (B) DS, (C) indented 10 spaces from the left margin only. 2. _____
3. The body of a report is (A) SS, (B) DS, (C) TS. 3. _____
4. The author-date format includes the author's last name and the year of publication followed by (A) a comma and the page number, (B) a colon and the page number, (C) a comma and the title of the work. 4. _____
5. Page one of an unbound report has (A) 1½″, (B) 2″, (C) 1″ side margins. 5. _____
6. If a source has two authors, give for a reference (A) the last name of the author who is listed first, (B) both last names joined by the word *and*, (C) the last name of one author followed by et al. 6. _____

© by the Glencoe Division of Macmillan/McGraw-Hill.

7. When more than one work by the same author is used, give for a reference (A) the first name or initial of the author, (B) the complete title of the work, (C) a shortened version of the title. 7. _____

8. On the continuing pages of an unbound report, the body of the report begins on (A) line 9 and is DS, (B) line 8 and is DS, (C) line 7 and is SS. 8. _____

9. Return/enter (A) 2 times, (B) 3 times, (C) 4 times after the name of the author on page one of an unbound report. 9. _____

10. A standard-size (8½" × 11") sheet of paper has (A) 51 lines, (B) 56 lines, (C) 66 lines. 10. _____

E M 10. To move the cursor directly to the beginning or ending of a document, page, or line, use (A) prompt, (B) express cursor moves, (C) format commands. 10. _____

Completion

Complete each statement at the right by writing the correct word, number, or phrase in the blank.

1. A ________________ page for a report contains the title of the report, the author's name, the name of the course, and the date.
2. All pages after the first page of a report are known as ________________.
3. Side margins for page one of an unbound report are ______ inch(es).
4. A quotation of ______ or fewer lines is keyed within the normal paragraph text and is enclosed within quotation marks.
5. The ________________ is an alphabetic listing of all the sources referred to or used by the writer in preparing a report.
6. ________________ is the vertical and horizontal arrangement of a page.
7. On the reference page, ________________ space the lines of each entry and ________________ space between entries.
8. Side margins for continuing pages of an unbound report are ______ inch(es).
9. A ________________ in the body of a report identifies the factual information taken from a specific source.
10. The page number on continuing pages of an unbound report is keyed ______ spaces before the right margin.

© by the Glencoe Division of Macmillan/McGraw-Hill.

OFFICE
SOFTWARE
SPECIALISTS

357 El Cajon Boulevard
San Diego, CA 92104

© by the Glencoe Division of Macmillan/McGraw-Hill.

OFFICE SOFTWARE SPECIALISTS

357 El Cajon Boulevard
San Diego, CA 92104

OFFICE
SOFTWARE
SPECIALISTS

357 El Cajon Boulevard
San Diego, CA 92104

© by the Glencoe Division of Macmillan/McGraw-Hill.

OFFICE SOFTWARE SPECIALISTS

357 El Cajon Boulevard
San Diego, CA 92104

OFFICE
SOFTWARE
SPECIALISTS

357 El Cajon Boulevard
San Diego, CA 92104

© by the Glencoe Division of Macmillan/McGraw-Hill.

OFFICE SOFTWARE SPECIALISTS

357 El Cajon Boulevard
San Diego, CA 92104

DATABASE
MANAGEMENT CONSULTANTS, INC.
Ten Forest Avenue, Wilmore, KY 40390

© by the Glencoe Division of Macmillan/McGraw-Hill.

DATABASE
MANAGEMENT CONSULTANTS, INC.

Ten Forest Avenue, Wilmore, KY 40390

Solutions

Word Scale Practice (pp. 11–12)

Activity 1	Activity 2
1. 8	1. 64
2. 48	2. 124
3. 14	3. 37
4. 27	4. 84
5. 46	5. 56

Activity 3	Activity 4
1. 55	1. 57
2. 89	2. 44
3. 39	3. 56
4. 59	4. 61

Misstroke Location Practice (pp. 13–14)

Activity 1 Omitted Letter(s)

Joe quicly proofread three term paers.
Reaching agreemen was a real necesity.
Janice needed mor time or keyboarding.

Activity 2 Omitted Word(s)

Ms. Brandt will another test today.
Yes, she finished assignments early.
Paul gave her one apple two peaches.

Activity 3 Added Letter(s)

The computer printout willl ben due today.
Too gain skill, your must always practice.
Do not forget too let Barb know thee rule.

Activity 4 Added Word(s)

The disk is not not currently in in this drive.
Andy knew his his answers were were all accurate.
Tanya left as as soon as she she finished work.

Activity 5 Review of Activities 1–4

As you input information, try concenrate on your workk. When your wanders, you tend to to make errrors. Emploers usuallly expect a employee too produce doccuments that are error freee. Correctting errors time cconsuming. Having spent timen makin correctionss can result lower productivity. Lower producttivity often resullts in lower profit for for the employe. Profit is important too any employer. No employer wil permit an employyee to contrbute to lowerin profits indefiniteely.

Activity 6 Extra Space

To re duce mis strokes, use concentra tion.
Per fect practice of fers perfect result s.
Concen tration is neces sary for accuracy.

Activity 7 No Space

Karl always usedgood keying techniques.
Eliminatefatigue by usinggood posture.
Always letyour eyes remain onthebook.

Activity 8 Misstroke

Johm proofreed carifully to find errers.
Make neet corrections on als misstroles.
Find and corrict tee 10 mistrokes here.

Activity 9 Transposition

Accurate keying si required for hte job.
Your wokr is always naet and error fere.
Taek pride daily ni het work yuo produce.

Activity 10 Strikeover

Set high standards and work toward them.
You'll feel proud when you reach a goal.
Set goals which reflect these standards.

Activity 11 Review of Activities 6–9

You should always planyour assignment befere you begin. This mens taking tim to reed your instfuctions ande gather material and supplies you'l nead. Make cetrain yuo under stand all aspects fo the jbo beforebeginning work. You can waset valuabel tine and effort fi you haev to redo a job because youdid not underatand wha t het task involvde. Effective emploeyes adk questions to claer up nay prob lems beforethey begin to werk no a take. Understanding what needs to bedone before startnig is veyr important. Youmight be very embarrassde and furstrated wneh you have todo a jbo again simply be cause you failedto under stand all the instrcutions.

Goal Writing Practice (pp. 15–16)

Activity 1

Keting by touch means that you arecapable of striking the keys with out looking at your fingers. A distinctive Trait of outstanding keyboarders si their ability to by key touch.

You should presently be keying nearly al of your work by touch. Seldom should you have to to glance at your fingers Instances when you have to look down should be few and far between.

1' | 1 | 2 | 3 | 4 | 5 | 6 | 7 | 8 | 9 | 10
3' | 1 | 2 | 3

GWAM 1' 73 Accuracy 1' 86.3
3' 24 3' 60

© by the Glencoe Division of Macmillan/McGraw-Hill.

Activity 2

advances in technology have changed teh job market. Some fields foemployment have been eliminated while others have ben created.

What the world of work will be like in the year to come will depend on the changes in Technology. When you select a careertry to chose one that will allowsome flexibility to meet the changes in technology.

1' 1 2 3 4 5 6 7 8 9 10
3' 1 2 3

GWAM 1' 70 Accuracy 1' 86.8
3' 23 3' 64

Activity 3

Computer systems are made up of sevreal components; computer, keyboard, screen, printer, and disk drive. The key-board is used to enter data in to the computer. Data may be viewed on the screen or sent to to the printer. Data is store on floppy disks using the Disk drive. A computer system is useful only when you have Software that tells the computer what to do.

1' 1 2 3 4 5 6 7 8 9 10
3' 1 2 3

GWAM 1' 73 Accuracy 1' 87.7
3' 24 3' 64

Activity 4

A Typical day for a social worker involves helping people identify and to solve their problems. To be effective, a social worker must be sensitive, yet objective at the same time.

A bachelor's degree is often needed for entry level jobs. Many states give School grants to to thoose workers who want to earn masters' degree and to advance in their careers.

1' 1 2 3 4 5 6 7 8 9 10 11
3' 1 2 3 4

GWAM 1' 72 Accuracy 1' 87.7
3' 24 3' 64

Language Arts (pp. 19–26)

Activity 1
Practice

1. liti-gant Rule 2
2. perma-nent Rule 2
3. imperi-alism Rule 3
4. month Rule 1
5. iden-tity Rule 3

1. mis-spelled Rule 2
2. bar-gain Rule 2
3. upon Rule 1
4. prac-tice Rule 2
5. ency-clopedia Rule 3
6. chair Rule 1
7. oven Rule 1
8. gal-lery Rule 2
9. folder Rule 3
10. liv-ery Rule 2
11. excel-lent Rule 3
12. potas-sium Rule 2

Activity 2
Practice

1. self-denial Rule 5
2. March 17, 1990 Rule 4
3. $509,831 Rule 4
4. Joe Duggan, Ph.D. Rule 4
5. out-field Rule 5

1. pres-ently Rule 2
2. San Francisco Rule 4
3. must Rule 1
4. their Rule 1
5. per-fect Rule 2
6. after-noon Rule 5
7. California's Rule 4
8. in-triguing Rule 2
9. Fisherman's Rule 4
10. sour-dough Rule 5
11. "S.F." Rule 4
12. Gate Rule 1

© by the Glencoe Division of Macmillan/McGraw-Hill.

Activity 3

Practice

1. zucchini, Johnsons' Farm
2. sale, Clarke's Department Store
3. typewriters, printers
4. Paul Roberts, Louise Cohen, Toledo
5. company, Cohen and Bornstein, Inc.

1. Mary Johnson, California
2. Zebra
3. Juan, Peter
4. documents, Shoreline Drive
5. business
6. Clients, states
7. Fox
8. reports, copies
9. Roberto Dardino
10. Gravina, Shea, Golden
11. Toby
12. Juanita, Cecelia Jones
13. All, tickets, refunds
14. staff, desks, computers
15. Ms. Jennings, Mr. Allin

Activity 4

Practice

1. Monday, August 1, Friday, August 5
2. Maple Tree Nursery
3. True Typewriters, Inc.
4. Labor Day, Monday, September
5. the Book Port

1. Monday, October 2
2. Starlight Construction Company
3. Additions, Etc.
4. Friday, August 14
5. Starlight Construction Company
6. Additions, Etc.
7. Starline Construction Company
8. Franklin Press
9. O. J. Printing
10. Monday
11. Labor Day, Monday, September
12. September
13. Quick Print, Inc.
14. Print

Activity 5

Practice

1. two, its, to
2. It's, too
3. too
4. it's, its
5. its (two), to

1. it's
2. too
3. its
4. to
5. to
6. its
7. to
8. its
9. two
10. too
11. It's
12. too
13. to
14. to
15. two
16. it's
17. to

Activity 6

Practice

1. their (your, our), hour
2. are, your
3. our (their, your), there

1. their
2. they're
3. are
4. hours
5. There
6. are
7. you're
8. you're
9. their
10. Our
11. are
12. there
13. they're
14. are
15. their

Activity 7

Practice

1. "Learning Is Easy"
2. The Human Brain
3. "Would you be able," she asked, "to make my plane reservations?"

"After the disaster we had last year at the fall conference," Mr. Clarke began, "we will be better prepared this year for our fall sales conference." Mrs. Smith agreed and sugggested that everyone attending the conference read "Windows on the World," which appeared in the July issue of Window Magic. Ms. Kelly remarked, "The Chicago Daily and Architectural Advantages are highly recommended reading. Building Your Own Home, which is a television series on Channel 11 every Saturday afternoon, would also be helpful for everyone to watch." Mr. Clarke questioned whether anyone had read Mrs. Burrow's article, "Windows: The Allure of the Outdoors" or seen the movie, Opening Up Your Home? Although no one had either read the article or seen the movie, most of the people present said that they would try to do one or the other. All the sales representatives and sales managers present agreed to be better prepared for the fall conference; and to prove it, they all started singing the company song, "Windows are Better Than Doors to the World Outdoors."

© by the Glencoe Division of Macmillan/McGraw-Hill.

Review 1

1. your, Monday, January
2. "A Summer's Day," Young Writers
3. their, too
4. Our, Garden Restaurant
5. bicycle, to, you're
6. "When are you moving to your new apartment?"
7. "Computers in Schools," The Norfolk Gazette
8. typewriters, Memorial Day
9. their, our
10. report, Wednesday, July

Review 2

The library is a wonderful resource that is underused. It's very often overlooked by too many people. Almost every town has a library, and it's available to everyone. Are you using your library to its fullest? There are many resources in it. Books and magazines are available at your library, as well as local newspapers, such as The Milton Daily. If you asked your librarian, "Please help me find the book Iguanas in St. Thomas," he or she could probably help you find it. Most libraries are open Monday through Saturday, except for holidays, such as Memorial Day and Thanksgiving.

Libraries can help you when you're looking for a job. Books such as The Occupational Outlook Handbook can help you discover what you might like to do and what sort of future you would find in various fields. Also, most libraries keep some annual reports from a number of companies. It's too easy to overlook your library. Librarians unite in saying, "Please use your library."

Proofreading Practice (pp. 36–40)

Activity 1

1. He needs $1,401,750 for this year's salary raises.
   He need $1,401,705 for this years' salary raises.
2. Have you submitted your entry for the poetry fair?
   Have you submited your entrx for thepoetry fair?
3. Please finish the order today. It must be mailed.
   Please finish teh order today, it must be mailed.
4. Did you apply for the position at the new company?
   Hid you apply for the postiion at the new comapny?
5. Professor Duhamel will speak to the class Tuesday.
   Professro duhamle will spek to the class Teusday.
6. Do all of you have dictionaries readily available?
   Doall fo you have dictionries readdily available?

Activity 2

1. Who will be the next famous guest speaker for you?
   Who will be the nxt famouf guest speakre for you?
2. Are there computers here that I could use Tuesday?
   Are their computers here tht I could use Teusday?
3. The books must be balanced by the end of the week.
   The boks mustbe ballanced by the end of this week

4. Kay keyed one letter, five memos, and six reports.
   Kay keyed on letter five memos and six repotrs.
5. Learning to write is not as difficult as it seems.
   Learning write to is not as difficult sa it seems.
6. The bill for the paper for $54.69 is due March 17.
   The bil for the paper for $4569 is do March 17.

Activity 3

1. Not alike	6. Not alike
2. Alike	7. Not alike
3. Not alike	8. Not alike
4. Not alike	9. Alike
5. Not alike	10. Not alike

Activity 4

1. B	6. A
2. All alike	7. All alike
3. A, C	8. B, C
4. A	9. A, C
5. A, B	10. C

Activity 5

	Sale Figures	
Salesperson	1988	1999
D. Pickerign	$37,089	$39,422
M. Cole	29,641	31,200
K. Wu	34,102	35,800
T. Bohorquz	41,768	42,999

Activity 6

There si no need to to be a "wallflower" when your in agroup. You cna become part if teh conversaition without bein overbearing. If you you are het type of person who say nothing in group situation it's easy easy to over come ths hangup. In word, it's enthusiasm. when you are a in converversation, shift your thinkin in to hgh gear and git excited about what's beeing discussed. Then you'll automatically speek yp adn be abl to ad to the the converation.

Fear is comon whn you're inolved in a conversation The easiest way to rise above teh fi to steer you thinking away from your fears. As your thinking vecomes more posipositive dna consturctive, your prsonalty wil automaticaly takeon a new tone.

Activity 7

Novermber 17, 19--

Mr. Mark O'Leary
Offices, Incorporated
77 ParkSquare
New York, NY 10007

Dear Ms. O'Leary

Your publicatoin called Office furniture is veery innformative. Thanks yuo fro sendding it us to.
i think that I will order our neew offic desks form you

I would, however like to seea sampel of the regal deks. Do yo hvae of any theese Desks available for veiwing I wwould be able to examine thesse desks ayn monday tuesday or wednesday during the nxet few weks.

since We aer anxous to placeour ordre, pleas call me soon at 721-6790. I forward to heering form yoo.

Very Truly Yours

Meredith MacIntosh
purchsing managre

Activity 8

January 4, 19--

Ms. Rebecca Levy
H. T. Construction Compnay
4201 east street
Asn Francisco, CA 94188

Dear Ms. Levy

The First phasse fo construction tion on the medcial Lab looks excellent. Every one seem thrilledwith teh nwe setup. is the completion date february 17

Becuase schedlling of, please letus now the the beginning adn Endng dates fro the seecond phas by mondy, janyuary 11.

We have ben verry Pleasedwith your wokr, adn we antcipate uisng T. H. construction again in the futture.

Sincerly yours

Roger cullen
Asistant Managager

© by the Glencoe Division of Macmillan/McGraw-Hill.